VEGETABLES

Vegetables

13-Digit ISBN: 978-1-64643-063-5
10-Digit ISBN: 1-64643-063-8

This book may be ordered by mail from the publisher. Please include $5.99 for postage and handling. Please support your local bookseller first!

Books published by Cider Mill Press Book Publishers are available at special discounts for bulk purchases in the United States by corporations, institutions, and other organizations. For more information, please contact the publisher.

Cider Mill Press Book Publishers
"Where good books are ready for press"
PO Box 454
12 Spring Street
Kennebunkport, Maine 04046

Visit us online!
cidermillpress.com

Typography: Adobe Garamond Pro, Black Jack, Gotham, Type Embellishments One

Image Credits: Photos on pages 11, 35, 44, 48, 63, 67, 75, 93, 101, 109, 110, 113, 115, 116, 119, 125, 126, 136, 139, 140, 143, 144, 147, 151, 155, 156, 159, 160, 163, 168, 171, 172, 175, 181, 182, 189, 193, 194, 197, 201, 205, 206, 209, 219, 220, 228, 235, and 237 courtesy of Cider Mill Press. All other images used under official license from Shutterstock.com.

Front cover image:
Stuffed Eggplants, see page 230.

Back cover image:
Ratatouille, see page 203.

Front endpaper image:
Peppers Stuffed with Feta, Olive & Basil Salad, see page 104.

Back endpaper image:
Roasted Corn & Red Pepper Soup, see page 133.

Printed in China
1 2 3 4 5 6 7 8 9 0
First Edition

VEGETABLES

Over 100 Vegetable-Forward Recipes

CIDER MILL
PRESS

BOOK
PUBLISHERS
KENNEBUNKPORT, MAINE

TABLE *of* CONTENTS

❧ ❈ ❧

INTRODUCTION

Though the role of vegetables in our diet has come a long way and farmers markets have started to pop up in places where they were once unthinkable, there remain plenty who fear taking a step or two back from the rich meals that center around meat. Envisioning nothing but a boring string of salads lining up to greet them, these unfortunate souls are kept ignorant of the wondrous flavors and innovative preparations that Mother Nature and the contemporary culinary revolution have joined forces to make available.

This book intends to open everyone's eyes to those possibilities. Having scanned the globe for a collection of dishes that attain a level of excellence, emphasize freshness, and highlight vegetables and varietals that are often overlooked, *Vegetables* promises to make each trip to the supermarket's produce section or the local farm stand charged with the excitement a child feels when set loose in a candy store.

To be clear, this book is not vegetarian, but vegetable-centric. The times that meat does appear it is most commonly as a flavoring agent rather than a central component—those familiar with Chinese cuisine will recognize the approach straight off.

Flavor is always the top concern when constructing a cookbook, with health coming in a close second. Deciding to go for the green in your diet means that you'll be distancing yourself from the processed foods responsible for so many of the chronic diseases that have become a large issue in the contemporary world.

Considering that you'll feel better and more energetic, and vastly improve your palate, committing to a plant-based diet suddenly seems like a no-brainer.

CHAPTER 1

SNACKS &

SIDES

Traditionally, a snack centered around veggies means a platter of crudités flanked by a rich, sour cream–based dip that squashes the flavor of the produce. As this book intends to convince you that a new day has dawned, it makes sense to revolutionize the idea of what a vegetable can do when you need a small bite with big flavor.

As we've all spent the entire month of November dreaming about the Thanksgiving meal, what vegetables can do as a side dish requires no revolution. From the assertive flavors of a roasted brassica to the lighter greens that require nothing more than a steam bath to grow toothsome, the preparations in the second piece of this chapter are certain to round out any table.

Beet Chips

INGREDIENTS

5 BEETS, PEELED AND SLICED
VERY THIN

¼ CUP OLIVE OIL

2 TEASPOONS KOSHER SALT

DIRECTIONS

1. Preheat the oven to 400°F. Place the beets and olive oil in a bowl and toss until the slices are evenly coated. Place them on parchment-lined baking sheets in a single layer. Place the beets in the oven and bake for 12 to 15 minutes, or until crispy.

2. Remove the chips from the oven and sprinkle the salt over them. Serve warm or store in an airtight container for up to 1 week.

YIELD: **4 SERVINGS**

ACTIVE TIME: **15 MINUTES**

TOTAL TIME: **20 MINUTES**

Fried Taro Strips

INGREDIENTS

VEGETABLE OIL, AS NEEDED

1 LARGE TARO ROOT, PEELED AND JULIENNED

SALT, TO TASTE

ANCHO CHILI POWDER, TO TASTE

2 TABLESPOONS FRESH LIME JUICE

DIRECTIONS

1. Add vegetable oil to a Dutch oven until it is 2 or 3 inches deep. Warm the oil to 350°F over medium-high heat.

2. Add the taro root and fry until golden brown, about 5 minutes. Make sure not to crowd the pot and work in batches if necessary.

3. Transfer the fries to a large bowl. Sprinkle the salt and chili powder over them and drizzle the lime juice on top. Toss until the fries are evenly coated and serve.

YIELD: **4 SERVINGS**

ACTIVE TIME: **20 MINUTES**

TOTAL TIME: **20 MINUTES**

Bhaji

INGREDIENTS

2 EGGS

3 LARGE RED ONIONS, SLICED
INTO THIN HALF-MOONS

1 CUP ALL-PURPOSE FLOUR

1 TEASPOON CORIANDER

1 TEASPOON CUMIN

1 SERRANO PEPPER, STEMMED,
SEEDS AND RIBS REMOVED,
AND MINCED

½ TEASPOON KOSHER SALT

1 CUP VEGETABLE OIL, PLUS MORE
AS NEEDED

DIRECTIONS

1. Place the eggs in a bowl and whisk until scrambled. Add the onions, flour, coriander, cumin, serrano pepper, and salt and stir to combine.

2. Place the vegetable oil in an 8-inch cast-iron skillet and warm over medium heat. When it starts to shimmer, add a large spoonful of the onion batter and fry until golden brown, about 30 to 45 seconds. Turn the fritter over and fry until it is crisp and golden brown all over, about 30 seconds. Transfer to a paper towel–lined plate to drain. Repeat with the remaining batter, adding and heating more oil if it starts to run low. When all of the fritters have been cooked, serve immediately.

NOTE: These fritters can be varied in dozens of ways. Try adding shredded carrot, chilies, a bit of coconut, or even threads of parsnip to get an idea of what else you might like to incorporate.

Muthia with Cilantro Yogurt

INGREDIENTS

FOR THE MUTHIA

1 TABLESPOON KOSHER SALT

1 GREEN CABBAGE, OUTER LEAVES RESERVED, REMAINDER CORED AND CHOPPED

1½ CUPS CHICKPEA FLOUR, PLUS MORE AS NEEDED

2 TABLESPOONS COCONUT OIL, MELTED

2-INCH PIECE OF FRESH GINGER, PEELED AND MINCED

2 TABLESPOONS MINCED FRESNO CHILI PEPPER

1 TABLESPOON CORIANDER

1½ TEASPOONS CUMIN

½ TEASPOON TURMERIC

1½ TEASPOONS KOSHER SALT

FOR THE YOGURT

1 CUP FRESH CILANTRO LEAVES

1 CUP BABY SPINACH

¼ CUP COLD WATER

2 CUPS PLAIN YOGURT

PINCH OF CAYENNE PEPPER

DIRECTIONS

1. To begin preparations for the muthia, fill a Dutch oven with water and bring it to a boil. Prepare an ice water bath as the water warms. Add the salt and chopped cabbage to the boiling water and cook for 1 minute. Use a strainer to transfer the cabbage to the ice water bath. After 1 minute, drain the cabbage and squeeze it to remove as much liquid as possible. Place on a kitchen towel to dry. Keep the water in the Dutch oven.

2. Place the chickpea flour and coconut oil in a bowl and stir to combine. Add the cabbage and the remaining ingredients and stir until the dough starts to hold together. Place the dough on a flour-dusted work surface and knead until it is smooth and stiff. Divide the dough into 18 pieces and roll them into balls.

3. Place 1 inch of water in a large pot and place a steaming tray in the pot. Line the steaming tray with the reserved cabbage leaves and place the dumplings in the tray. Bring the water to a boil and steam the dumplings until they are shiny and firm, about 20 minutes.

4. While the dumplings are steaming, prepare the yogurt. Return the water in the Dutch oven to a boil and prepare another ice water bath. Add the cilantro and spinach to the boiling water, cook for 1 minute, drain, and transfer the cilantro and spinach to the ice water bath. Drain, squeeze to remove as much liquid from the mixture as possible, and transfer the mixture to a food processor. Add the water and half of the yogurt to the food processor and puree until smooth. Place this mixture, the cayenne pepper, and the remaining yogurt in a bowl, stir to combine, and serve alongside the steamed dumplings.

Punjabi Samosa

INGREDIENTS

FOR THE WRAPPERS

2 CUPS MAIDA FLOUR, PLUS MORE
AS NEEDED

¼ TEASPOON KOSHER SALT

2 TABLESPOONS OLIVE OIL

½ CUP WATER, PLUS MORE
AS NEEDED

FOR THE FILLING

2 RUSSET POTATOES, PEELED
AND CHOPPED

2 TABLESPOONS OLIVE OIL

1 TEASPOON CORIANDER SEEDS,
CRUSHED

½ TEASPOON FENNEL SEEDS,
CRUSHED

PINCH OF FENUGREEK SEEDS,
CRUSHED

1-INCH PIECE OF FRESH GINGER,
PEELED AND MINCED

1 GARLIC CLOVE, MINCED

Continued...

DIRECTIONS

1. To begin preparations for the wrappers, place the flour and salt in a mixing bowl and use your hands to combine them. Add the oil and work the mixture with your hands until it is a coarse meal. Add the water and knead the mixture until a smooth, firm dough forms. If the dough is too dry, incorporate more water 1 tablespoon at a time. Cover the bowl with a kitchen towel and set aside.

2. To begin preparations for the filling, place the potatoes in a saucepan and cover with water. Bring the water to a boil and cook until fork-tender, about 20 minutes. Transfer to a bowl, mash until smooth, and set aside.

3. Place the olive oil in a skillet and warm over medium heat. Add the crushed seeds and cook until fragrant, about 1 minute. Add the ginger, garlic, and jalapeño, sauté for 2 minutes, and then add the chili powder, coriander, turmeric, amchoor powder, and garam masala. Cook for another minute before adding the mashed potatoes and the curry leaves. Stir to combine, season with salt, transfer the mixture to a bowl, and let it cool completely.

4. Divide the dough for the wrappers into 8 pieces and roll each one out into a 6-inch circle on a flour-dusted work surface. Cut the circles in half and brush the flat edge of each piece with water. Fold one corner of the flat edge toward the other to make a cone and pinch to seal. Fill each cone one-third of the way with the filling, brush the opening with water, and pinch to seal. Place the sealed samosas on a parchment-lined baking sheet.

Continued...

1 TEASPOON MINCED
JALAPEÑO PEPPER

2 TEASPOONS CHILI POWDER

2 TABLESPOONS CORIANDER

¾ TEASPOON TURMERIC

1 TABLESPOON AMCHOOR POWDER

½ TEASPOON GARAM MASALA

6 CURRY LEAVES, MINCED

SALT, TO TASTE

VEGETABLE OIL, AS NEEDED

5. Add vegetable oil to a Dutch oven until it is 3 inches deep
and warm it to 325°F. Working in batches, add the filled
samosas to the hot oil and fry, turning them as they cook,
until they are golden brown, about 5 minutes. Transfer
the cooked samosas to a paper towel–lined plate and
serve once they have all been cooked.

*NOTE: Maida flour is finely milled to remove all of the bran
from the wheat, producing a soft result that closely resembles
cake flour.*

Zucchini Fritters

INGREDIENTS

1½ LBS. ZUCCHINI

SALT AND PEPPER, TO TASTE

¼ CUP ALL-PURPOSE FLOUR

¼ CUP GRATED PARMESAN CHEESE

1 EGG, BEATEN

3 TABLESPOONS OLIVE OIL

DIRECTIONS

1. Line a colander with cheesecloth and grate the zucchini into the colander. Generously sprinkle salt over the zucchini, stir to combine, and let sit for 1 hour. After 1 hour, press down on the zucchini to remove as much liquid from it as you can.

2. Place the zucchini, flour, Parmesan, and egg in a mixing bowl and stir to combine. Use your hands to form handfuls of the mixture into balls and then gently press down on the balls to form them into patties.

3. Place the oil in a cast-iron skillet and warm it over medium-high heat. When the oil starts to shimmer, place the patties in the skillet, taking care not to crowd the skillet and working in batches if necessary. Cook until golden brown, about 5 minutes. Flip them over and cook for another 5 minutes, until the fritters are also golden brown on that side.

4. Remove the fritters from the skillet, transfer to a paper towel–lined plate, and repeat with the remaining patties. When all of the fritters have been cooked, season with salt and pepper and serve.

YIELD: **4 SERVINGS**

ACTIVE TIME: **15 MINUTES**

TOTAL TIME: **24 HOURS**

Spicy Chickpeas

INGREDIENTS

1 CUP DRIED CHICKPEAS, SOAKED OVERNIGHT AND DRAINED

2 CUPS VEGETABLE OIL

1 TEASPOON SMOKED PAPRIKA

½ TEASPOON ONION POWDER

½ TEASPOON BROWN SUGAR

¼ TEASPOON GARLIC POWDER

¼ TEASPOON KOSHER SALT

PINCH OF CHILI POWDER

DIRECTIONS

1. Bring water to a boil in a saucepan. Add the chickpeas, reduce heat so that the water simmers, and cook until the chickpeas are tender, about 40 minutes. Drain the chickpeas, place them on a paper towel–lined plate, and pat them dry.

2. Place the oil in a Dutch oven and warm it to 350°F over medium heat.

3. Place the remaining ingredients in a bowl, stir until thoroughly combined, and set the mixture aside.

4. Place the chickpeas in the hot oil and fry until golden brown, about 3 minutes. Remove and place in the bowl with the seasoning mixture. Toss to coat and serve.

Minty Pickled Cucumbers

YIELD: **2 CUPS**

ACTIVE TIME: **20 MINUTES**

TOTAL TIME: **3 HOURS**

INGREDIENTS

½ CUP SUGAR

½ CUP WATER

½ CUP RICE VINEGAR

2 TABLESPOONS DRIED MINT

1 TABLESPOON CORIANDER SEEDS

1 TABLESPOON MUSTARD SEEDS

2 CUCUMBERS, SLICED

DIRECTIONS

1. Place all of the ingredients, except for the cucumbers, in a small saucepan and bring to a boil, stirring to dissolve the sugar.

2. Place the cucumbers in a large mason jar. When the sugar has dissolved, remove the pan from heat and pour the brine over the cucumbers. Let cool completely before using or storing in the refrigerator, where the pickles will keep for 1 week.

YIELD: **4 SERVINGS**

ACTIVE TIME: **5 MINUTES**

TOTAL TIME: **15 MINUTES**

Kale Chips

INGREDIENTS

1 BUNCH OF KALE, STEMMED

1 TEASPOON KOSHER SALT

½ TEASPOON BLACK PEPPER

½ TEASPOON PAPRIKA

½ TEASPOON DRIED PARSLEY

½ TEASPOON DRIED BASIL

¼ TEASPOON DRIED THYME

¼ TEASPOON DRIED SAGE

2 TABLESPOONS OLIVE OIL

DIRECTIONS

1. Preheat the oven to 400°F. Tear the kale leaves into smaller pieces and place them in a mixing bowl. Add the remaining ingredients and work the mixture with your hands until the kale pieces are evenly coated.

2. Divide the seasoned kale between two parchment-lined baking sheets so that it sits on each in an even layer. Place in the oven and bake until crispy, 6 to 8 minutes. Remove and let cool before serving.

Roasted Artichoke & Spinach Dip

YIELD: **1 CUP**

ACTIVE TIME: **5 MINUTES**

TOTAL TIME: **15 MINUTES**

INGREDIENTS

¾ LB. ARTICHOKE HEARTS, QUARTERED

4 GARLIC CLOVES

2 CUPS BABY SPINACH

2 TABLESPOONS APPLE CIDER VINEGAR

¼ TEASPOON KOSHER SALT

¼ CUP OLIVE OIL

PINCH OF ONION POWDER (OPTIONAL)

DIRECTIONS

1. Preheat the oven's broiler to high. Place the artichoke hearts on a baking sheet and broil, turning them occasionally, until browned all over, about 10 minutes.

2. Place the artichoke hearts and the remaining ingredients in a food processor and blitz until the desired texture of the spread is achieved.

YIELD: **4 SERVINGS**

ACTIVE TIME: **20 MINUTES**

TOTAL TIME: **30 MINUTES**

Zucchini Rolls

INGREDIENTS

3 SMALL ZUCCHINI, SLICED THIN
LENGTHWISE

2 TABLESPOONS OLIVE OIL

SALT AND PEPPER, TO TASTE

3 TABLESPOONS GOAT CHEESE

1 TABLESPOON FINELY CHOPPED
FRESH PARSLEY

½ TEASPOON FRESH LEMON JUICE

2 OZ. BABY SPINACH, FINELY
CHOPPED

3 TABLESPOONS PINE NUTS

FRESH BASIL, FINELY CHOPPED,
TO TASTE

DIRECTIONS

1. Preheat your gas or charcoal grill to medium heat (about 400°F). Brush the zucchini slices with the olive oil and season them with salt and pepper.

2. Place the zucchini on the grill and cook until charred on both sides and tender, about 8 minutes.

3. Place the goat cheese, parsley, and lemon juice in a bowl and stir to combine.

4. Spread the goat cheese mixture over the grilled zucchini. Sprinkle the spinach, pine nuts, and basil over the spread and then roll the slices up. Secure the rolls with toothpicks and serve.

YIELD: **2 CUPS**

ACTIVE TIME: **5 MINUTES**

TOTAL TIME: **5 MINUTES**

Olive Tapenade

INGREDIENTS

1½ CUPS CURED BLACK OR
KALAMATA OLIVES, PITTED

1 TEASPOON WHITE MISO PASTE

3 TABLESPOONS CAPERS, RINSED

1½ TABLESPOONS FINELY CHOPPED
FRESH PARSLEY

3 GARLIC CLOVES

3 TABLESPOONS FRESH
LEMON JUICE

¼ TEASPOON BLACK PEPPER, PLUS
MORE TO TASTE

¼ CUP OLIVE OIL

SALT, TO TASTE

DIRECTIONS

1. Place the olives, miso paste, capers, parsley, garlic, lemon juice, and black pepper in a food processor and pulse until coarsely chopped.

2. Drizzle the olive oil into the mixture and pulse a few more times until a chunky paste forms, scraping down the work bowl as needed. Season with salt and pepper and serve.

Tiropitakia

INGREDIENTS

½ LB. FETA CHEESE

1 CUP GRATED KEFALOTYRI CHEESE

¼ CUP FINELY CHOPPED FRESH PARSLEY

2 EGGS, BEATEN

BLACK PEPPER, TO TASTE

1 (1 LB.) PACKAGE OF FROZEN PHYLLO DOUGH, THAWED

2 STICKS OF UNSALTED BUTTER, MELTED

DIRECTIONS

1. Place the feta cheese in a mixing bowl and break it up with a fork. Add the kefalotyri, parsley, eggs, and pepper and stir to combine. Set the mixture aside.

2. Place 1 sheet of the phyllo dough on a large sheet of parchment paper. Gently brush the sheet with some of the melted butter, place another sheet on top, and brush this with more of the butter. Cut the phyllo dough into 2-inch-wide strips, place 1 teaspoon of the filling at the end of the strip closest to you, and fold over one corner to make a triangle. Fold the strip up until the filling is completely covered. Repeat with the remaining sheets of phyllo dough and filling.

3. Preheat the oven to 350°F and oil a baking sheet with some of the melted butter. Place the pastries on the baking sheet and bake in the oven until golden brown, about 15 minutes. Remove and let cool briefly before serving.

HUMMUS VARIATIONS

For a more authentic hummus, soak dried chickpeas overnight and then cook them until tender. You can also dress this hummus up with any of the following options: add 1 to 3 teaspoons of spices like cumin, sumac, harissa, or smoked paprika; blend in 1 cup of roasted eggplant, zucchini, bell peppers, or garlic; or fold in ¾ cup of chopped green or black olives.

Traditional Hummus

INGREDIENTS

1 (14 OZ.) CAN OF CHICKPEAS, DRAINED AND LIQUID RESERVED

3 TABLESPOONS OLIVE OIL

3 TABLESPOONS TAHINI

1½ TABLESPOONS FRESH LEMON JUICE, PLUS MORE TO TASTE

1 GARLIC CLOVE, CHOPPED

1 TEASPOON KOSHER SALT

½ TEASPOON BLACK PEPPER

DIRECTIONS

1. If time allows, remove the skins from each of the chickpeas. This will make your hummus much smoother.

2. Place the chickpeas, olive oil, tahini, lemon juice, garlic, salt, and pepper in a food processor and blitz until the mixture is very smooth, scraping down the work bowl as needed.

3. Taste and adjust the seasoning. If your hummus is more stiff than you'd like, add 2 to 3 tablespoons of the reserved chickpea liquid and blitz until it is the desired consistency.

YIELD: **1 CUP**

ACTIVE TIME: **10 MINUTES**

TOTAL TIME: **25 MINUTES**

Basil Pesto

INGREDIENTS

¼ CUP PINE NUTS

3 GARLIC CLOVES

SALT AND PEPPER, TO TASTE

2 CUPS FIRMLY PACKED FRESH
BASIL LEAVES

½ CUP OLIVE OIL

¼ CUP GRATED PARMESAN CHEESE

¼ CUP GRATED PECORINO SARDO
CHEESE

DIRECTIONS

1. Warm a small skillet over low heat for 1 minute. Add the pine nuts and cook, while stirring, until they begin to give off a toasty fragrance, 2 to 3 minutes. Transfer to a plate and let cool completely.

2. Place the garlic, salt, and pine nuts in a food processor or blender and pulse until the mixture is a coarse meal. Add the basil and pulse until finely minced. Transfer the mixture to a bowl and add the oil in a thin stream as you quickly whisk it in.

3. Add the cheeses and stir until thoroughly incorporated. The pesto will keep in the refrigerator for up to 4 days and in the freezer for up to 3 months.

YIELD: **4 CUPS**

ACTIVE TIME: **30 MINUTES**

TOTAL TIME: **3 TO 7 DAYS**

Kimchi

INGREDIENTS

1 HEAD OF NAPA CABBAGE, CUT INTO STRIPS

½ CUP KOSHER SALT

2-INCH PIECE OF FRESH GINGER, PEELED AND MINCED

3 GARLIC CLOVES, MINCED

1 TEASPOON SUGAR

5 TABLESPOONS RED PEPPER FLAKES

3 BUNCHES OF SCALLIONS, TRIMMED AND SLICED

WATER, AS NEEDED

DIRECTIONS

1. Place the cabbage and salt in a large bowl and stir to combine. Wash your hands, or put on gloves, and work the mixture with your hands, squeezing to extract as much liquid as possible from the cabbage. Let the mixture rest for 2 hours.

2. Add the remaining ingredients, except for the water, work the mixture with your hands until well combined, and squeeze to extract as much liquid as possible.

3. Transfer the mixture to a large mason jar and press down so it is tightly packed together. The liquid should be covering the mixture. If it is not, add water until the mixture is covered.

4. Cover the jar and let the mixture sit at room temperature for 3 to 7 days, removing the lid daily to release the gas that has built up.

YIELD: **20 TORTILLAS**

ACTIVE TIME: **30 MINUTES**

TOTAL TIME: **1 HOUR**

Corn Tortillas

INGREDIENTS

2 CUPS MASA HARINA, PLUS MORE
AS NEEDED

½ TEASPOON KOSHER SALT

1 CUP WARM WATER (110°F),
PLUS MORE AS NEEDED

2 TABLESPOONS VEGETABLE OIL

DIRECTIONS

1. Place the masa harina and salt in a bowl and stir to combine. Slowly add the warm water and oil and stir until they have been incorporated and a soft dough forms. The dough should be quite soft and not at all sticky. If it is too dry, add more water. If the dough is too wet, add more masa harina. Wrap the dough in plastic and let it rest at room temperature for 30 minutes. The dough can also be stored in the refrigerator for up to 24 hours.

2. Warm a cast-iron skillet over medium-high heat. Pinch off a small piece of the dough and roll it into a ball. Place the ball between two pieces of parchment paper or plastic wrap and use a large cookbook (or something of similar weight) to flatten the ball into a thin disk.

3. Place the disk in the skillet and cook until brown spots begin to appear, about 45 seconds. Flip the disk over, cook for 1 minute, and transfer the cooked tortilla to a plate. Cover with a kitchen towel and repeat with the remaining dough.

NOTE: Masa harina is a very fine flour that is made from hominy or corn kernels that have been cooked and soaked in a diluted solution of calcium hydroxide—aka limewater—before being milled.

Roasted Brussels Sprouts with Bacon, Blue Cheese & Pickled Red Onion

YIELD: **4 SERVINGS**

ACTIVE TIME: **15 MINUTES**

TOTAL TIME: **50 MINUTES**

INGREDIENTS

1 CUP CHAMPAGNE VINEGAR

1 CUP WATER

½ CUP SUGAR

2 TEASPOONS KOSHER SALT, PLUS MORE TO TASTE

1 SMALL RED ONION, SLICED

½ LB. BACON, CHOPPED

1½ LBS. BRUSSELS SPROUTS, TRIMMED AND HALVED

BLACK PEPPER, TO TASTE

4 OZ. BLUE CHEESE, CRUMBLED

DIRECTIONS

1. Place the vinegar, water, sugar, and salt in a saucepan and bring to a boil. Place the onion in a bowl and pour the boiling liquid over the slices. Cover and allow to cool completely.

2. Place the bacon in a large sauté pan and sauté over medium heat until crisp, about 7 minutes. Transfer the bacon to a paper towel–lined plate and leave the rendered fat in the pan.

3. Place the Brussels sprouts in the pan, cut side down, season with salt and pepper, and cook over medium heat until they are a deep golden brown, about 7 minutes.

4. Transfer the Brussels sprouts to a serving dish, top with the pickled onions, bacon, and blue cheese and serve.

Carrot & Jicama Slaw

INGREDIENTS

½ LB. CARROTS, PEELED

½ LB. JICAMA, PEELED

2 TABLESPOONS FRESH LIME JUICE

1 TABLESPOON OLIVE OIL

¼ TEASPOON ANCHO CHILI POWDER

¼ CUP CHOPPED FRESH CILANTRO

SALT, TO TASTE

DIRECTIONS

1. Grate the carrots and jicama, place them in a mixing bowl, and add the remaining ingredients. Stir until combined.

2. Taste, adjust seasoning if necessary, and serve.

TOASTED SEED GRANOLA

Preheat the oven to 300°F. Place 1 tablespoon real maple syrup, 2 tablespoons honey, brown sugar, and butter, and 1 teaspoon kosher salt in a small saucepan and warm over medium heat, stirring until the brown sugar has dissolved. Place 1½ cups oats in a mixing bowl, add the honey mixture, and stir until the oats are evenly coated. Transfer to a parchment-lined baking sheet, place it in the oven, and bake for 40 minutes, stirring the mixture every 10 minutes to ensure it bakes evenly. Remove from the oven and let the granola cool slightly. Transfer to a mixing bowl, fold in ½ cup dried cranberries and ¾ cup toasted pumpkin seeds, and serve.

Spicy Baby Carrots with Toasted Seed Granola

YIELD: **4 SERVINGS**

ACTIVE TIME: **30 MINUTES**

TOTAL TIME: **1 HOUR AND 45 MINUTES**

INGREDIENTS

2 LBS. BABY CARROTS

2 TABLESPOONS OLIVE OIL

1½ TABLESPOONS KOSHER SALT, PLUS 1½ TEASPOONS

1 TEASPOON BLACK PEPPER

2 TEASPOONS CUMIN

1 TEASPOON GROUND FENNEL

1 TEASPOON CORIANDER

1 TEASPOON PAPRIKA

2 TEASPOONS BROWN SUGAR

2 CUPS PLAIN GREEK YOGURT

2 TABLESPOONS HONEY

1½ TEASPOONS FINELY CHOPPED THYME, PLUS MORE FOR GARNISH

½ CUP TOASTED SEED GRANOLA (SEE SIDEBAR)

DIRECTIONS

1. Preheat the oven to 375°F. Place the carrots, olive oil, 1½ tablespoons of salt, pepper, cumin, fennel, coriander, paprika, and brown sugar in a bowl and toss to coat evenly. Arrange the carrots in an even layer on an aluminum foil–lined baking sheet. Place the carrots in the oven and roast until tender, about 25 minutes. Remove and let cool slightly.

2. Place the yogurt, honey, remaining salt, and thyme in a serving dish and stir to combine. Place the carrots on top and sprinkle the granola over the carrots. Garnish with additional thyme and serve.

Southern Collard Greens

INGREDIENTS

2 TABLESPOONS OLIVE OIL

1 ONION, DICED

½ LB. SMOKED HAM OR BACON, DICED

4 GARLIC CLOVES, DICED

3 LBS. COLLARD GREENS, STEMMED AND CHOPPED

2 CUPS VEGETABLE STOCK (SEE PAGE 140)

¼ CUP APPLE CIDER VINEGAR

1 TABLESPOON BROWN SUGAR

1 TEASPOON RED PEPPER FLAKES

DIRECTIONS

1. Place the oil in a Dutch oven and warm it over medium-high heat. When the oil starts to shimmer, add the onion and sauté until it is translucent, about 3 minutes.

2. Add the ham or bacon and cook over medium heat until it starts to brown. Stir in the remaining ingredients, cover the pot, and braise the collard greens for about 2 hours, or until they are extremely tender. Check on the collard greens every so often and add water if all of the liquid evaporates, so the greens do not burn.

Browned Fennel with Orange Glaze

YIELD: **4 SERVINGS**

ACTIVE TIME: **20 MINUTES**

TOTAL TIME: **30 MINUTES**

INGREDIENTS

2 TABLESPOONS OLIVE OIL

2 LARGE FENNEL BULBS, TRIMMED AND QUARTERED

⅔ CUP FRESH ORANGE JUICE

1 TEASPOON FENNEL SEEDS

1 TABLESPOON UNSALTED BUTTER

SALT, TO TASTE

DIRECTIONS

1. Place the oil in a saucepan and warm it over medium heat. When the oil starts to shimmer, add the fennel, cut side down, and cook until it is well browned, about 8 minutes. Turn and let the other sides brown.

2. Add the orange juice and fennel seeds and gently deglaze the pan, scraping up any browned bits from the bottom. Cover the pan and let the fennel braise for 5 minutes.

3. Remove the lid and cook until the juice reduces and becomes syrupy. Add the butter, stir until melted, season with salt, and serve.

Kale with Garlic & Raisins

YIELD: **4 SERVINGS**

ACTIVE TIME: **10 MINUTES**

TOTAL TIME: **25 MINUTES**

INGREDIENTS

1 TABLESPOON OLIVE OIL

½ LB. LACINATO OR RED RUSSIAN KALE, STEMMED AND CHOPPED

2 GARLIC CLOVES, MINCED

¼ CUP RAISINS

¼ CUP WATER

SALT AND PEPPER, TO TASTE

LEMON WEDGES, FOR SERVING

DIRECTIONS

1. Place the olive oil in a large skillet and warm it over medium heat. When the oil starts to shimmer, add the kale and sauté until it starts to soften, about 5 minutes.

2. Stir in the garlic and sauté until it starts to brown, about 1 minute. Add the raisins and water, stirring constantly, and cook until the water has evaporated, about 5 minutes.

3. Season with salt and pepper and serve with the lemon wedges.

Sautéed Radicchio with Beans, Parmesan & Balsamic

YIELD: **4 SERVINGS**

ACTIVE TIME: **1 HOUR**

TOTAL TIME: **24 HOURS**

INGREDIENTS

⅔ CUP DRIED BEANS, SOAKED OVERNIGHT

1 TABLESPOON OLIVE OIL

1 SMALL HEAD OF RADICCHIO, CORED AND SLICED THIN

1 SHALLOT, MINCED

1 GARLIC CLOVE, MINCED

¼ CUP WHITE WINE

¼ CUP VEGETABLE STOCK (SEE PAGE 140)

SALT AND PEPPER, TO TASTE

½ TEASPOON FINELY CHOPPED FRESH THYME

PARMESAN CHEESE, GRATED, FOR GARNISH

BALSAMIC VINEGAR, TO TASTE

DIRECTIONS

1. Drain the beans and rinse them with cold water. Place them in a pot, cover with water, and bring to a boil. Reduce the heat so that the beans simmer and cook until tender, about 40 minutes. Remove from heat and let cool.

2. Place the oil in a skillet and warm over medium heat. When the oil starts to shimmer, add the radicchio and sauté until it starts to wilt and brown, about 5 minutes. Stir in the shallot and garlic and sauté until the garlic starts to brown, about 2 minutes. Deglaze the pan with the wine and stock.

3. Drain the beans and add them to the radicchio mixture along with salt and pepper and the thyme. Cook until almost all of the liquid has evaporated and then remove the pan from heat. Top with Parmesan and balsamic vinegar and serve.

NOTE: If you have an infused balsamic vinegar, this dish is a perfect opportunity to break it out.

Yu Choy with Garlic & Soy

YIELD: **4 SERVINGS**

ACTIVE TIME: **10 MINUTES**

TOTAL TIME: **15 MINUTES**

INGREDIENTS

1½ LBS. YU CHOY (HALVED IF ESPECIALLY LONG)

¼ CUP WATER

1 TABLESPOON OLIVE OIL

2 GARLIC CLOVES, CHOPPED

1½ TEASPOONS RICE VINEGAR

1 TABLESPOON SOY SAUCE

DIRECTIONS

1. Place the yu choy in a pan large enough to fit all of it, cover with the water, cover the pan, and cook over high heat.

2. After about 5 minutes, check the thickest piece of yu choy to see if it is tender. If not, continue cooking.

3. Once tender, stir in the oil and garlic and sauté until the garlic is fragrant, about 1 minute.

4. Stir in the vinegar and soy sauce and serve.

Patatas Bravas

INGREDIENTS

2 CUPS WOOD CHIPS

4 POTATOES, CHOPPED

1 ONION WITH SKIN AND ROOT, HALVED

3 TABLESPOONS OLIVE OIL

1 GARLIC BULB, TOP ½ INCH REMOVED

1 (14 OZ.) CAN OF DICED TOMATOES, DRAINED

1 TABLESPOON SWEET PAPRIKA

1 TABLESPOON SHERRY VINEGAR

SALT, TO TASTE

SOUR CREAM, FOR SERVING

DIRECTIONS

1. Place the wood chips in a bowl of cold water and let them soak for 30 minutes.

2. Bring water to a boil in a large saucepan. Add the potatoes and boil for 4 minutes. Drain and run the potatoes under cold water.

3. Place the potatoes, onion, and 1 tablespoon of the olive oil in a mixing bowl and toss to coat.

4. Line a large wok with aluminum foil, making sure that the foil extends over the side of the pan. Add the soaked wood chips and place the wok over medium heat.

5. When the wood chips are smoking heavily, place a wire rack above the wood chips and place the potatoes, onion, and garlic on top. Cover the wok with a lid, fold the foil over the lid to seal the wok as best you can, and smoke the vegetables for 20 minutes. After 20 minutes, remove the pan from heat and keep the wok covered for another 20 minutes.

6. Place the tomatoes, paprika, vinegar, and remaining olive oil in a blender and puree until smooth. Set the mixture aside.

7. Remove the garlic and onion from the wok. Peel and roughly chop them. Add them to the mixture in the blender and puree until smooth. Season the salsa brava with salt and serve alongside the smoked potatoes and sour cream.

Garlic & Chili Broccolini

YIELD: **4 SERVINGS**

ACTIVE TIME: **10 MINUTES**

TOTAL TIME: **20 MINUTES**

INGREDIENTS

SALT AND PEPPER, TO TASTE

½ LB. BROCCOLINI, TRIMMED

¼ CUP OLIVE OIL

2 GARLIC CLOVES, MINCED

1 TEASPOON RED PEPPER FLAKES

2 TABLESPOONS TOASTED ALMONDS, SLICED, FOR GARNISH

DIRECTIONS

1. Bring a large pot of water to a boil. Add salt and the broccolini and cook for 30 seconds. Remove the broccolini with a strainer, allow the majority of the water to drip off, and transfer to a paper towel–lined plate.

2. Place the olive oil in a large skillet and warm over medium-high heat. When the oil starts to shimmer, add the broccolini and cook until it is well browned. Turn the broccolini over, add the garlic, season with salt and pepper, and toss to combine. When the broccolini is browned all over, stir in the red pepper flakes and toss to evenly distribute. Garnish with the toasted almonds and serve.

YIELD: **4 SERVINGS**

ACTIVE TIME: **20 MINUTES**

TOTAL TIME: **25 MINUTES**

Mom's Creamed Spinach

INGREDIENTS

1 TABLESPOON UNSALTED BUTTER

1 YELLOW ONION, CHOPPED

2 GARLIC CLOVES, CHOPPED

1 LB. FROZEN SPINACH

½ LB. CREAM CHEESE, AT ROOM TEMPERATURE

PINCH OF FRESHLY GRATED NUTMEG

1 TEASPOON DRIED MARJORAM

SALT AND PEPPER, TO TASTE

DIRECTIONS

1. Place the butter in a skillet and melt it over medium heat. Add the onion and garlic and sauté until the onion is translucent, about 3 minutes.

2. Add the spinach to the pan along with a few teaspoons of water, cover the pan, and cook for 4 minutes. Remove the lid, break the spinach up with a wooden spoon, and cook until it is completely thawed.

3. Stir in the cream cheese, nutmeg, and marjoram and cook until the sauce has thickened, about 5 minutes. Season with salt and pepper and serve.

NOTE: Make sure you use frozen spinach for this one, as fresh will wilt and leave you with far less than the amount you need to bring to the table.

Grilled Corn with Chipotle Mayonnaise & Goat Cheese

YIELD: **4 SERVINGS**

ACTIVE TIME: **25 MINUTES**

TOTAL TIME: **1 HOUR AND 15 MINUTES**

INGREDIENTS

6 EARS OF CORN, IN THEIR HUSKS

3 CHIPOTLES IN ADOBO

½ CUP MAYONNAISE

¼ CUP SOUR CREAM

1½ TABLESPOONS BROWN SUGAR

1 TABLESPOON FRESH LIME JUICE

2 TABLESPOONS FINELY CHOPPED FRESH CILANTRO, PLUS MORE FOR GARNISH

1 TEASPOON KOSHER SALT, PLUS MORE TO TASTE

½ TEASPOON BLACK PEPPER, PLUS MORE TO TASTE

3 TABLESPOONS OLIVE OIL

½ CUP CRUMBLED GOAT CHEESE

6 LIME WEDGES, FOR SERVING

DIRECTIONS

1. Preheat the oven to 400°F. Place the ears of corn on a baking sheet, place it in the oven, and roast the corn for about 25 minutes, until the kernels have a slight give to them. Remove from the oven and let the corn cool. When the ears of corn are cool enough to handle, husk them and set aside.

2. Preheat a gas or charcoal grill to medium heat (about 400°F). Place the chipotles, mayonnaise, sour cream, brown sugar, lime juice, cilantro, salt, and pepper in a food processor and blitz until smooth. Set the mixture aside.

3. Drizzle the olive oil over the ears of corn, season with salt and pepper, and place them on the grill. Cook, while turning, until they are charred all over, about 10 minutes.

4. Spread the mayonnaise mixture over the ears of corn, sprinkle the goat cheese on top, and garnish with additional cilantro. Serve with the wedges of lime.

Fried Brussels Sprouts with Maple-Cider Glaze

YIELD: **4 SERVINGS**

ACTIVE TIME: **10 MINUTES**

TOTAL TIME: **15 MINUTES**

INGREDIENTS

¾ CUP REAL MAPLE SYRUP

½ CUP APPLE CIDER VINEGAR

½ CUP APPLE CIDER

SALT, TO TASTE

VEGETABLE OIL, AS NEEDED

1 LB. BRUSSELS SPROUTS, TRIMMED AND HALVED

DIRECTIONS

1. Place the maple syrup, vinegar, apple cider, and a pinch of salt in a saucepan and cook, stirring constantly, over medium heat until the mixture has reduced by one-quarter. Remove the pan from heat and set aside.

2. Add oil to a Dutch oven until it is about 3 inches deep. Warm it to 350°F, place the Brussels sprouts in the oil, and fry until they are crispy and browned, about 1 to 2 minutes. Transfer to a paper towel–lined plate to drain.

3. Place the Brussels sprouts in a bowl, season with salt, and add 1 tablespoon of the glaze for every cup of Brussels sprouts. Toss until evenly coated and serve.

TIP: If you prefer not to deep-fry the Brussels sprouts, toss them with oil and salt and roast at 375°F for 20 minutes, until they are just tender.

Potato & Celeriac Gratin with Gruyère & Figs

YIELD: **4 SERVINGS**

ACTIVE TIME: **30 MINUTES**

TOTAL TIME: **1 HOUR AND 30 MINUTES**

INGREDIENTS

1½ LBS. RUSSET POTATOES, PEELED AND SLICED THIN

½ LB. CELERIAC, PEELED, TRIMMED, AND SLICED THIN

1 BAY LEAF

1 TEASPOON KOSHER SALT, PLUS MORE TO TASTE

2 GARLIC CLOVES, CRUSHED

2 TABLESPOONS MILK

1 TABLESPOON UNSALTED BUTTER

3 DRIED OR FRESH FIGS, CHOPPED

4 OZ. GRUYÈRE CHEESE, GRATED

PINCH OF FRESHLY GRATED NUTMEG

½ CUP HEAVY CREAM

DIRECTIONS

1. Preheat the oven to 375°F. Place the potatoes and celeriac in a medium saucepan and cover with water. Add the bay leaf, salt, the garlic, and milk, bring to a boil, and then reduce the heat to medium-low. Simmer for 1 minute and drain. Remove the bay leaf and discard it.

2. Butter an oval gratin dish or a casserole dish and add half of the potatoes and celeriac, making sure they are evenly distributed. Sprinkle half of the figs, Gruyère, and nutmeg on top, season with salt, and repeat with the remaining potatoes, celeriac, figs, Gruyère, and seasonings.

3. Pour the cream over the top and cover the dish with aluminum foil. Place it in the oven and bake for 20 minutes. Remove the foil and bake for another 15 minutes, until the top is browned and most of the liquid has cooked off.

4. Remove the gratin from the oven and let it stand for 15 minutes before serving.

YIELD: **4 SERVINGS**

ACTIVE TIME: **15 MINUTES**

TOTAL TIME: **20 MINUTES**

Savory Halwa

INGREDIENTS

2 TABLESPOONS UNSALTED BUTTER

1 LB. CARROTS, PEELED AND GRATED

½ TEASPOON CARDAMOM

2 CUPS MILK

SALT, TO TASTE

DIRECTIONS

1. Place the butter in a saucepan and melt over medium heat. Add the carrots and cardamom and sauté until the carrots start to soften, about 5 minutes.

2. Add the milk, bring the mixture to a simmer, and cook until the milk has reduced and the carrots are very tender, about 10 minutes. Season with salt and serve.

NOTE: This preparation is a twist on a traditional Indian dessert. If you're interested in trying the sweeter version, add ¼ cup brown sugar along with the milk.

YIELD: **4 SERVINGS**

ACTIVE TIME: **20 MINUTES**

TOTAL TIME: **1 HOUR AND 15 MINUTES**

Cauliflower Gratin

INGREDIENTS

2 CUPS WHITE WINE

2½ CUPS WATER

⅓ CUP KOSHER SALT

2 STICKS OF UNSALTED BUTTER

6 GARLIC CLOVES, CRUSHED

2 SHALLOTS, HALVED

1 CINNAMON STICK

3 WHOLE CLOVES

1 TEASPOON BLACK PEPPERCORNS

1 SPRIG OF FRESH SAGE

2 SPRIGS OF FRESH THYME

1 HEAD OF CAULIFLOWER, TRIMMED

1 CUP SHREDDED EMMENTAL CHEESE

¼ CUP GRATED PARMESAN CHEESE

DIRECTIONS

1. Place all of the ingredients, except for the cauliflower and cheeses, in a large saucepan and bring to a boil. Reduce the heat so that the mixture gently simmers, add the head of cauliflower, and poach it until tender, about 30 minutes.

2. While the cauliflower is poaching, preheat the oven to 450°F. Transfer the cauliflower to a baking sheet, place it in the oven, and bake until the top is a deep golden brown, about 10 minutes.

3. Remove the cauliflower from the oven and spread the cheeses evenly over the top. Return to the oven and bake until the cheeses have browned. Remove from the oven and let cool slightly before slicing the cauliflower into quarters and serving.

YIELD: **4 SERVINGS**

ACTIVE TIME: **35 MINUTES**

TOTAL TIME: **45 MINUTES**

Pommes Anna

INGREDIENTS

3 TABLESPOONS UNSALTED BUTTER

1 LB. SWEET POTATOES, PEELED AND SLICED THIN

1 LB. PURPLE-TOP TURNIPS, PEELED, TRIMMED, AND SLICED THIN

1 TEASPOON FINELY CHOPPED FRESH THYME

SALT, TO TASTE

DIRECTIONS

1. Warm a 10- to 12-inch skillet over medium heat. Melt 1 tablespoon of the butter and remove the pan from heat. Place one slice of sweet potato along the edge of the pan, followed by a turnip slice. Continue along the edge, alternating slices of sweet potato and turnip. When the outside edge is complete, make another row in the inner circle and then in the very center.

2. Sprinkle half of the thyme and a pinch of salt on top. Make another layer with the remaining slices of sweet potato and turnip and top with the thyme and salt.

3. Dot the top with another tablespoon of butter, place the pan on the stove, and cook over low heat for 5 minutes. Cover the pan with a lid and continue to cook.

4. Remove the lid every 5 minutes to let out steam. Check on the bottom layer after roughly 20 minutes by gently lifting with a spatula. If it isn't browning, remove the lid and continue cooking. If nice and brown, find a plate with flat edges that is the same size as your pan. With one hand on the pan's handle and another on the plate, carefully invert the vegetables onto the plate, then gently slide the veggies back into the pan, browned side up. Add the remaining butter if the pan seems dry.

5. Cook until tender all the way through, about 10 minutes. To serve, either invert onto a serving plate or, if it holds in one piece, lift it out with a spatula.

Hasselback Sweet Potatoes with Lime & Cilantro

YIELD: **4 SERVINGS**

ACTIVE TIME: **15 MINUTES**

TOTAL TIME: **1 HOUR**

INGREDIENTS

4 SWEET POTATOES

6 TABLESPOONS UNSALTED BUTTER, AT ROOM TEMPERATURE

1 LIME, QUARTERED

¼ CUP FINELY CHOPPED FRESH CILANTRO

DIRECTIONS

1. Preheat the oven to 450°F. While taking care not to cut through the last ¼ inch, cut the sweet potatoes into thin slices. Place the potatoes on a baking sheet, spread the butter over them, and place them in the oven. Roast until fork-tender, 30 to 40 minutes.

2. Remove from the oven, squeeze a wedge of lime over each sweet potato, sprinkle the cilantro on top, and serve.

YIELD: **4 SERVINGS**

ACTIVE TIME: **20 MINUTES**

TOTAL TIME: **35 MINUTES**

Succotash

INGREDIENTS

1 TABLESPOON OLIVE OIL

1 LB. MUSHROOMS, STEMMED
AND SLICED

1 RED ONION, MINCED

4 CUPS CORN KERNELS

1 RED BELL PEPPER, STEMMED,
SEEDS AND RIBS REMOVED,
AND CHOPPED

2 CUPS EDAMAME

1 TABLESPOON UNSALTED BUTTER

SALT AND PEPPER, TO TASTE

1 TABLESPOON FINELY CHOPPED
FRESH MARJORAM

½ CUP FINELY CHOPPED
FRESH BASIL

DIRECTIONS

1. Place the olive oil in a large cast-iron skillet and warm it over medium heat. When the oil starts to shimmer, add the mushrooms and sauté until they release their liquid and start to brown, about 10 minutes. Reduce the heat to low and cook until the mushrooms are a deep brown, about 15 minutes.

2. Add the onion, raise the heat to medium-high, and sauté until it starts to soften, about 5 minutes. Add the corn, bell pepper, and edamame and sauté until the edamame is tender, about 8 minutes.

3. Add the butter and stir until it has melted and coated all of the vegetables. Season with salt and pepper, add the marjoram and basil, stir to incorporate, and serve.

Lemon Cauliflower Rice

INGREDIENTS

1 HEAD OF CAULIFLOWER, CHOPPED

2 TABLESPOONS OLIVE OIL

SALT, TO TASTE

3 TABLESPOONS FRESH LEMON JUICE

2 TEASPOONS LEMON ZEST

DIRECTIONS

1. Place the pieces of cauliflower in a food processor and blitz until granular.

2. Place the olive oil in a skillet and warm it over medium-high heat. When the oil starts to shimmer, add the cauliflower and cook, stirring occasionally, until it starts to brown, about 8 minutes.

3. Season the cauliflower with salt, stir in the lemon juice and lemon zest, and cook, stirring occasionally, until the "rice" is fragrant and warmed through, about 4 minutes.

Roasted Roots with Ras el Hanout & Honey

YIELD: **4 SERVINGS**

ACTIVE TIME: **10 MINUTES**

TOTAL TIME: **45 MINUTES**

INGREDIENTS

4 LARGE PARSNIPS, PEELED, TRIMMED, CORED, AND CHOPPED

4 LARGE CARROTS, PEELED AND SLICED LENGTHWISE

2 TABLESPOONS OLIVE OIL

SALT AND PEPPER, TO TASTE

2 TABLESPOONS HONEY

1 TABLESPOON RAS EL HANOUT

DIRECTIONS

1. Preheat the oven to 400°F. Place the parsnips and carrots in a baking pan in one layer, drizzle the olive oil over the mixture, and season with salt and pepper. Stir to combine, place the pan in the oven, and roast for about 25 minutes, or until the vegetables are starting to brown.

2. Remove the pan from the oven and move the vegetables into a pile in the center of the tray. Drizzle the honey over the pile and stir until the vegetables are evenly coated. Sprinkle the ras el hanout over the vegetables and stir until evenly distributed.

3. Return the pan to the oven and roast the vegetables for another 5 to 10 minutes, until the vegetables are well browned and cooked through. Remove from the oven and let the vegetables cool briefly before serving.

YIELD: **4 SERVINGS**

ACTIVE TIME: **25 MINUTES**

TOTAL TIME: **40 MINUTES**

Taro Ulass

INGREDIENTS

½ CUP VEGETABLE STOCK
(SEE PAGE 140)

JUICE FROM ½ LEMON

1 LB. TARO ROOT, PEELED
AND CUBED

1 LARGE BUNCH OF RED CHARD,
STEMS AND LEAVES SEPARATED
AND CHOPPED

½ BUNCH OF FRESH CILANTRO,
CHOPPED

1 TABLESPOON OLIVE OIL

2 GARLIC CLOVES, CHOPPED

DIRECTIONS

1. Place the stock, lemon juice, and taro in a saucepan, bring to a simmer over medium heat, and cook until the taro is tender, about 8 minutes. Remove the pan from heat and set it aside.

2. Place the chard leaves and the cilantro in a pan containing approximately ¼ cup water. Cook over medium heat until the chard is wilted and most of the liquid has evaporated. Transfer the mixture to a food processor and blitz until pureed.

3. Place the olive oil in a large skillet and warm over medium heat. When the oil starts to shimmer, add the garlic and the chard stems and sauté until the garlic starts to brown, about 1 minute. Stir in the taro mixture and the chard puree, cook until heated through, and serve.

YIELD: **4 SERVINGS**

ACTIVE TIME: **15 MINUTES**

TOTAL TIME: **40 MINUTES**

Bamies

INGREDIENTS

OLIVE OIL, AS NEEDED

1 ONION, CHOPPED

1 LB. OKRA, RINSED WELL
AND CHOPPED

1 POTATO, PEELED AND MINCED

1 GARLIC CLOVE, MINCED

2 TOMATOES, CHOPPED

3 TABLESPOONS WHITE WINE

½ CUP VEGETABLE STOCK
(SEE PAGE 140)

2 TABLESPOONS FINELY CHOPPED
FRESH PARSLEY

2 TEASPOONS SUGAR

SALT, TO TASTE

FETA CHEESE, CRUMBLED,
FOR GARNISH

DIRECTIONS

1. Place the oil in a large skillet and warm over medium heat. When the oil starts to shimmer, add the onion and sauté until it starts to brown, about 8 minutes. Add the okra and potato and cook, stirring continuously, until they start to brown, about 5 minutes.

2. Add the garlic and cook for 1 minute. Stir in the tomatoes, wine, stock, parsley, and sugar and cook until the tomatoes have completely collapsed and the okra and potato are tender, about 8 minutes. Season with salt, garnish with feta, and serve immediately.

CHAPTER 2

SALADS

---

*In terms of flexibility, freshness, and speed, a salad is unmatched.
But far too often a lack of inspiration and imagination makes salad feel
like a concession of defeat rather than a cause for celebration.*

*These salads will help switch the salad from its default position to something
desirable. Whether you're looking for a light first course or something
substantial enough to serve as a main, you're certain to find it here.*

Chili, Shrimp & Basil Salad

YIELD: **6 SERVINGS**

ACTIVE TIME: **20 MINUTES**

TOTAL TIME: **20 MINUTES**

INGREDIENTS

FOR THE DRESSING

2 RED BIRD'S EYE CHILI PEPPERS

½ CUP SOY SAUCE

½ CUP SAMBAL OELEK

JUICE FROM 3 LIMES

¼ CUP BROWN SUGAR

1-INCH PIECE OF FRESH GINGER, PEELED AND MINCED

2 TABLESPOONS CURRY POWDER

Continued...

DIRECTIONS

1. To prepare the dressing, place all of the ingredients in a food processor and blitz until smooth. Set aside.

2. To prepare the salad, place all of the ingredients, except for the cashews, in a mixing bowl and stir to combine. Add the dressing, toss to coat, top with the cashews, and serve.

FOR THE SALAD

½ HEAD OF NAPA CABBAGE,
CHOPPED

1 CUP FRESH MINT LEAVES,
CHOPPED

2 CUPS FRESH BASIL LEAVES,
CHOPPED

1 CUP FRESH CILANTRO, CHOPPED

1 RED ONION, SLICED THIN

3 SCALLIONS, TRIMMED AND
SLICED THIN

1 CARROT, PEELED AND
SLICED THIN

1 LB. SHRIMP, COOKED
AND CHOPPED

¼ CUP CASHEWS, CHOPPED,
FOR GARNISH

Horiatiki Salad

INGREDIENTS

1 CUCUMBER, PEELED, SEEDED, AND SLICED INTO HALF-MOONS

1 CUP CHERRY TOMATOES, HALVED

1 CUP CRUMBLED FETA CHEESE

1 ONION, CHOPPED

½ CUP KALAMATA OLIVES, PITTED AND SLICED

1 TEASPOON DRIED OREGANO

½ CUP OLIVE OIL

SALT AND PEPPER, TO TASTE

DIRECTIONS

1. Place the cucumber, cherry tomatoes, feta, onion, olives, and dried oregano in a mixing bowl and toss to gently until combined.

2. Drizzle the olive oil over the salad, season with salt and pepper, and gently toss to combine.

YIELD: **4 SERVINGS**

ACTIVE TIME: **5 MINUTES**

TOTAL TIME: **5 MINUTES**

Carrot & Mint Salad

INGREDIENTS

3 CARROTS, PEELED AND
JULIENNED

1 TABLESPOON OLIVE OIL

1 TABLESPOON APPLE CIDER
VINEGAR

¾ TEASPOON CUMIN

2 TABLESPOONS FINELY CHOPPED
FRESH MINT

SALT AND PEPPER, TO TASTE

DIRECTIONS

1. Place all of the ingredients in a mixing bowl and stir
   gently until combined.

Lentil Salad

INGREDIENTS

4 CUPS WATER

1 CUP LENTILS, PICKED OVER AND RINSED

2½ TABLESPOONS WHITE WINE VINEGAR

3 GARLIC CLOVES, MINCED

1 TEASPOON HERBES DE PROVENCE

1 BAY LEAF

SALT AND PEPPER, TO TASTE

1 (14 OZ.) CAN OF CHICKPEAS, DRAINED AND RINSED

¾ LB. CHERRY TOMATOES, HALVED

1 RED ONION, SLICED

½ CUP FRESH PARSLEY, CHOPPED

¼ CUP OLIVE OIL

2 CUPS BABY SPINACH

½ CUP CRUMBLED FETA CHEESE

DIRECTIONS

1. Place the water, lentils, 1 tablespoon of the vinegar, the garlic, herbes de Provence, and bay leaf in a slow cooker and season with salt. Cover and cook on high until the lentils are tender, about 2 hours.

2. Drain the lentils, discard the bay leaf, transfer to a large salad bowl, and let the lentils cool.

3. When the lentils are cool, stir in all of the remaining ingredients, except for the feta, and toss to combine. Season with salt and pepper, sprinkle the feta on top of the salad, and serve.

Charred Brassica Salad with Buttermilk Caesar

YIELD: **4 SERVINGS**

ACTIVE TIME: **20 MINUTES**

TOTAL TIME: **45 MINUTES**

INGREDIENTS

FOR THE SALAD

1 SMALL HEAD OF CAULIFLOWER, TRIMMED AND CHOPPED

1 HEAD OF BROCCOLI, CUT INTO FLORETS

¼ CUP OLIVE OIL

4 OZ. BRUSSELS SPROUTS, TRIMMED AND HALVED

PICKLED RAMPS (SEE SIDEBAR)

RED PEPPER FLAKES, FOR GARNISH

PARMESAN CHEESE, GRATED, FOR GARNISH

FOR THE DRESSING

2 GARLIC CLOVES, MINCED

1 TEASPOON MISO PASTE

⅔ CUP MAYONNAISE

¼ CUP BUTTERMILK

¼ CUP GRATED PARMESAN CHEESE

ZEST OF 1 LEMON

1 TEASPOON WORCESTERSHIRE SAUCE

1 TEASPOON KOSHER SALT, PLUS MORE TO TASTE

½ TEASPOON BLACK PEPPER, PLUS MORE TO TASTE

DIRECTIONS

1. To begin preparations for the salad, bring a large pot of water to a boil. Add salt and the cauliflower, cook for 1 minute, remove the cauliflower with a slotted spoon, and transfer it to a paper towel–lined plate. Wait for the water to return to a boil, add the broccoli, and cook for 30 seconds. Use a slotted spoon to remove the broccoli and transfer it to the paper towel–lined plate.

2. Place the oil and Brussels sprouts, cut side down, in a large cast-iron skillet. Add the broccoli and cauliflower, season with salt and pepper, and cook over high heat, making sure not to move the vegetables, until charred. Turn the vegetables over and cook until charred on that side. Remove the mixture from the pan and transfer it to a salad bowl.

3. To prepare the dressing, place all of the ingredients in a food processor and blitz until combined. Taste and adjust the seasoning if necessary.

4. Add the Pickled Ramps and dressing to the salad bowl and toss to distribute. Garnish with Parmesan cheese and red pepper flakes and serve.

PICKLED RAMPS

Place ½ cup champagne vinegar, ½ cup water, ¼ cup sugar, 1½ teaspoons kosher salt, ¼ teaspoon fennel seeds, ¼ teaspoon coriander seeds, and ⅛ teaspoon red pepper flakes in a small saucepan and bring to a boil. Add 10 small ramp bulbs, reduce heat, and simmer for 1 minute. Transfer the contents of the saucepan to a mason jar, cover, and let cool completely before using or storing. The ramps will keep in the refrigerator for up to 1 week.

YIELD: **4 SERVINGS**

ACTIVE TIME: **20 MINUTES**

TOTAL TIME: **24 HOURS**

Chickpea Salad

INGREDIENTS

FOR THE SALAD

2 CUPS DRIED CHICKPEAS, SOAKED OVERNIGHT

4 CUPS CHICKEN STOCK (SEE PAGE 160)

1 CUP SUN-DRIED TOMATOES IN OLIVE OIL, DRAINED AND CHOPPED

1 ONION, CHOPPED

1 CUP FINELY CHOPPED FRESH CILANTRO

¼ CUP OLIVE OIL

¼ CUP FRESH LEMON JUICE

¼ TEASPOON SAFFRON

1 TABLESPOON CUMIN

1 TEASPOON CINNAMON

1 TEASPOON RED PEPPER FLAKES

SALT AND PEPPER, TO TASTE

DIRECTIONS

1. Drain the chickpeas, place them in a saucepan, and add the stock. Bring to a boil, reduce the heat, and simmer until the chickpeas are tender, about 40 minutes.

2. Drain the chickpeas and let them cool completely.

3. Place the chickpeas and the remaining ingredients in a mixing bowl, toss until combined, and serve.

Peppers Stuffed with Feta, Olive & Basil Salad

YIELD: **4 SERVINGS**

ACTIVE TIME: **10 MINUTES**

TOTAL TIME: **25 MINUTES**

INGREDIENTS

4 YELLOW BELL PEPPERS, SEEDED AND HALVED

12 CHERRY TOMATOES, HALVED

2 GARLIC CLOVES, MINCED

2 TABLESPOONS OLIVE OIL

½ CUP CRUMBLED FETA CHEESE

1 CUP BLACK OLIVES, PITTED

SALT AND PEPPER, TO TASTE

LEAVES FROM 1 BUNCH OF FRESH BASIL

DIRECTIONS

1. Preheat the oven to 375°F and place the peppers on a parchment-lined baking sheet.

2. Place the cherry tomatoes, garlic, olive oil, feta, and black olives in a mixing bowl and stir to combine. Divide the mixture between the peppers, place them in the oven, and roast until the peppers start to collapse, 10 to 15 minutes.

3. Remove the peppers from the oven and let them cool slightly. Season with salt and pepper and top with the basil leaves before serving.

Three-Bean Salad

INGREDIENTS

1 (14 OZ.) CAN OF KIDNEY BEANS, DRAINED AND RINSED

1 (14 OZ.) CAN OF CANNELLINI BEANS, DRAINED AND RINSED

1 (14 OZ.) CAN OF CHICKPEAS, DRAINED AND RINSED

1 GREEN BELL PEPPER, STEMMED, SEEDS AND RIBS REMOVED, AND CHOPPED

1 RED BELL PEPPER, STEMMED, SEEDS AND RIBS REMOVED, AND CHOPPED

½ CUCUMBER, CHOPPED

1 RED ONION, CHOPPED

1 CUP FRESH PARSLEY, CHOPPED

10 FRESH MINT LEAVES, TORN

10 FRESH BASIL LEAVES, TORN

FOR THE VINAIGRETTE

2 GARLIC CLOVES, MINCED

1½ TEASPOONS DIJON MUSTARD

2 TABLESPOONS FRESH LEMON JUICE

¼ CUP OLIVE OIL

SALT AND PEPPER, TO TASTE

DIRECTIONS

1. To prepare the salad, place all of the ingredients in a large salad bowl and toss to combine.

2. To prepare the vinaigrette, place all of the ingredients in a small bowl and whisk until combined.

3. Add the vinaigrette to the salad, toss to combine, and serve.

Couscous & Shrimp Salad

YIELD: **6 SERVINGS**

ACTIVE TIME: **40 MINUTES**

TOTAL TIME: **50 MINUTES**

INGREDIENTS

¾ LB. SHRIMP, SHELLED AND DEVEINED

6 BUNCHES OF FRESH MINT

10 GARLIC CLOVES, PEELED

3½ CUPS CHICKEN STOCK (SEE PAGE 160)

3 CUPS ISRAELI COUSCOUS

1 BUNCH OF ASPARAGUS, TRIMMED

3 PLUM TOMATOES, DICED

1 TABLESPOON FINELY CHOPPED FRESH OREGANO

½ ENGLISH CUCUMBER, DICED

ZEST AND JUICE OF 1 LEMON

½ CUP DICED RED ONION

½ CUP SUN-DRIED TOMATOES IN OLIVE OIL, DRAINED AND SLICED THIN

¼ CUP PITTED AND CHOPPED KALAMATA OLIVES

⅓ CUP OLIVE OIL

SALT AND PEPPER, TO TASTE

½ CUP CRUMBLED FETA CHEESE

DIRECTIONS

1. Place the shrimp, mint, and garlic in a Dutch oven and cover with water. Bring to a simmer over medium heat and cook until the shrimp are pink and cooked through, about 4 minutes after the water comes to a simmer. Drain, cut the shrimp in half lengthwise, and them set aside. Discard the mint and garlic cloves.

2. Place the stock in the Dutch oven and bring to a boil. Add the couscous, reduce the heat so that the stock simmers, cover, and cook until the couscous is tender and has absorbed the stock, 7 to 10 minutes. Transfer the couscous to a salad bowl.

3. Fill the pot with water and bring it to a boil. Add the asparagus and cook until it has softened, 1 to 1½ minutes. Drain, rinse under cold water, and chop into bite-sized pieces. Pat the asparagus dry.

4. Place all of the remaining ingredients, except for the feta, in the salad bowl containing the couscous. Add the asparagus and stir to incorporate. Top with the shrimp and the feta and serve.

Panzanella with White Balsamic Vinaigrette

YIELD: **6 SERVINGS**

ACTIVE TIME: **25 MINUTES**

TOTAL TIME: **45 MINUTES**

INGREDIENTS

FOR THE SALAD

1 TABLESPOON KOSHER SALT, PLUS 2 TEASPOONS

6 PEARL ONIONS, TRIMMED

1 CUP CORN KERNELS

1 CUP CHOPPED GREEN BEANS

4 CUPS CHOPPED DAY-OLD BREAD

2 CUPS CHOPPED OVERRIPE TOMATOES

10 LARGE FRESH BASIL LEAVES, TORN

BLACK PEPPER, TO TASTE

FOR THE VINAIGRETTE

½ CUP WHITE BALSAMIC VINEGAR

¼ CUP OLIVE OIL

2 TABLESPOONS MINCED SHALLOT

¼ CUP SLICED SCALLIONS

2 TABLESPOONS FINELY CHOPPED FRESH PARSLEY

2 TEASPOONS KOSHER SALT

1 TEASPOON BLACK PEPPER

DIRECTIONS

1. To begin preparations for the salad, bring water to a boil in a small saucepan and prepare an ice water bath. When the water is boiling, add the 1 tablespoon of salt and the pearl onions and cook for 5 minutes. When the onions have 1 minute left to cook, add the corn and green beans to the saucepan. Transfer the vegetables to the ice water bath and let them cool completely.

2. Remove the pearl onions from the water and squeeze to remove the bulbs from their skins. Cut the bulbs in half and break them down into individual petals. Drain the corn and green beans and pat the vegetables dry.

3. To prepare the vinaigrette, place all of the ingredients in a mixing bowl and whisk until combined.

4. Place the cooked vegetables, bread, tomatoes, and basil in a salad bowl and toss to combine. Add the remaining salt, season with pepper, and add half of the vinaigrette. Toss to coat and serve with the remaining vinaigrette on the side.

Spring Salad with Green Goddess Dressing

YIELD: **6 SERVINGS**

ACTIVE TIME: **20 MINUTES**

TOTAL TIME: **30 MINUTES**

INGREDIENTS

FOR THE DRESSING

½ CUP MAYONNAISE

⅔ CUP BUTTERMILK

1 TABLESPOON FRESH
LEMON JUICE

2 TABLESPOONS CHOPPED
CELERY LEAVES

2 TABLESPOONS CHOPPED
FRESH PARSLEY LEAVES

2 TABLESPOONS CHOPPED
FRESH TARRAGON

2 TABLESPOONS CHOPPED
FRESH CHIVES

2 TEASPOONS KOSHER SALT

1 TEASPOON BLACK PEPPER

Continued...

DIRECTIONS

1. To prepare the dressing, place all of the ingredients in a food processor and blitz until combined. Transfer to a container and place in the refrigerator until ready to serve.

2. To begin preparations for the salad, bring a pot of water to a boil and prepare an ice water bath in a large bowl. Add salt and the asparagus to the boiling water, cook for 1 minute, remove the asparagus with a strainer, and transfer it to the ice water bath until completely cool. Transfer to a kitchen towel to dry.

3. Place the peas in the boiling water, cook for 1 minute, remove with a strainer, and transfer to the water bath until completely cool. Transfer to a kitchen towel to dry.

4. Place one of the halved heads of lettuce on each serving plate. Place the asparagus and peas in a bowl, season with salt and pepper, and add half of the dressing. Toss to combine and place the mixture on top of the lettuce. Drizzle additional dressing over the top and garnish with the radish and celery leaves.

FOR THE SALAD

SALT AND PEPPER, TO TASTE

6 ASPARAGUS STALKS, TRIMMED
AND CHOPPED

4 OZ. SNAP PEAS, TRIMMED
AND CHOPPED

3 HEADS OF BABY RED LEAF
LETTUCE, HALVED

3 RADISHES, SLICED EXTREMELY
THIN WITH A MANDOLINE,
FOR GARNISH

CELERY LEAVES, FOR GARNISH

Shaved Squash Salad with Herb Vinaigrette

YIELD: **4 SERVINGS**

ACTIVE TIME: **15 MINUTES**

TOTAL TIME: **45 MINUTES**

INGREDIENTS

FOR THE SALAD

1 PINT CHERRY TOMATOES

1 TABLESPOON OLIVE OIL

5 GARLIC CLOVES, CRUSHED

1 TABLESPOON FINELY CHOPPED
FRESH THYME

½ TEASPOON KOSHER SALT, PLUS
MORE TO TASTE

¼ TEASPOON BLACK PEPPER, PLUS
MORE TO TASTE

3 ZUCCHINI, SLICED EXTREMELY
THIN WITH A MANDOLINE

2 SUMMER SQUASH, SLICED
EXTREMELY THIN WITH A
MANDOLINE

1 RED BELL PEPPER, STEMMED,
SEEDS AND RIBS REMOVED, AND
SLICED EXTREMELY THIN WITH
A MANDOLINE

Continued...

DIRECTIONS

1. To begin preparations for the salad, preheat the broiler on the oven to high. Place the cherry tomatoes, olive oil, garlic, thyme, salt, and pepper in a mixing bowl and toss until the tomatoes are evenly coated. Place the tomatoes on a baking sheet, place it in the oven, and broil until the skins begin to burst, 6 to 8 minutes. Remove from the oven and let cool completely.

2. To prepare the vinaigrette, place all of the ingredients, except for the olive oil, in a mixing bowl and whisk to combine. Add the oil in a slow stream while whisking to incorporate. Season to taste and set aside.

3. Place the zucchini, squash, and pepper in a large mixing bowl, season with salt and pepper, and add the vinaigrette. Toss to evenly coat, plate the salad, and sprinkle the blistered tomatoes over the top.

FOR THE VINAIGRETTE

1 TABLESPOON SLICED
FRESH CHIVES

1 TEASPOON FINELY CHOPPED
FRESH THYME

1 TEASPOON FINELY CHOPPED
FRESH OREGANO

1 TABLESPOON FINELY CHOPPED
FRESH PARSLEY

3 TABLESPOONS APPLE
CIDER VINEGAR

1 TABLESPOON HONEY

2 TEASPOONS DICED SHALLOT

1 TEASPOON KOSHER SALT

¼ TEASPOON BLACK PEPPER

¼ CUP OLIVE OIL

Chilled Corn Salad

INGREDIENTS

4 CUPS FRESH CORN KERNELS

2 TABLESPOONS UNSALTED BUTTER

1 JALAPEÑO PEPPER, STEMMED,
SEEDS AND RIBS REMOVED,
AND DICED

2 TABLESPOONS MAYONNAISE

2 TEASPOONS GARLIC POWDER

3 TABLESPOONS SOUR CREAM

¼ TEASPOON CAYENNE PEPPER

¼ TEASPOON CHILI POWDER

2 TABLESPOONS FETA CHEESE

2 TABLESPOONS COTIJA CHEESE

2 TEASPOONS FRESH LIME JUICE

½ CUP FINELY CHOPPED
FRESH CILANTRO

SALT AND PEPPER, TO TASTE

4 CUPS LETTUCE OR ARUGULA

DIRECTIONS

1. Preheat the oven to 400°F. Place the corn on a baking sheet, place it in the oven, and roast until the corn turns a light golden brown, about 35 minutes.

2. Remove the corn from the oven, let cool slightly, and then transfer to a large mixing bowl. Add all of the remaining ingredients, except for the lettuce or arugula, and stir to combine.

3. Place the salad in the refrigerator and chill overnight. When ready to serve, add the lettuce or arugula and stir to incorporate.

NOTE: If using canned, rather than fresh corn, you can skip roasting the kernels if you choose. If you want to roast them anyway, keep an eye on them after about 15 minutes, as they will not take nearly as long to cook.

YIELD: **4 SERVINGS**

ACTIVE TIME: **40 MINUTES**

TOTAL TIME: **1 HOUR AND 45 MINUTES**

Roasted Baby Beet Salad with Blue Cheese Mousse

INGREDIENTS

FOR THE SALAD

9 BABY BEETS (3 EACH OF RED, GOLDEN, AND PINK)

3 TABLESPOONS OLIVE OIL

1 TABLESPOON KOSHER SALT, PLUS MORE TO TASTE

9 SPRIGS OF FRESH THYME, LEAVES REMOVED FROM 3

6 GARLIC CLOVES

6 TABLESPOONS WATER

8 RADISHES WITH TOPS

6 OZ. BLUE CHEESE

½ CUP HEAVY CREAM

½ CUP RICOTTA CHEESE

2 APPLES, PEELED, CORED, AND DICED

BLACK PEPPER, TO TASTE

4 PIECES OF HONEYCOMB, FOR GARNISH

Continued...

DIRECTIONS

1. To begin preparations for the salad, preheat the oven to 400°F. Form three sheets of aluminum foil into pouches. Group the beets according to color and place each group into its own pouch. Drizzle the olive oil over each group and season with salt. Divide the whole sprigs of thyme, the garlic, and water between the pouches and seal them. Place the pouches on a baking sheet, place them in the oven, and roast until the beets are fork-tender, 45 minutes to 1 hour depending on the size of the beets. Remove the pouches from the oven and let cool. When cool enough to handle, peel the beets, cut them into bite-sized pieces, and set aside.

2. Bring a pot of water to a boil and prepare an ice water bath. Remove the greens from the radishes, wash them thoroughly, and set aside. Quarter the radishes. Add them and salt to the boiling water, cook for 2 minutes, and then transfer to the ice water bath.

3. Place the blue cheese, heavy cream, ricotta, and thyme leaves in a food processor and blitz until smooth. Set the mousse aside.

Continued...

FOR THE VINAIGRETTE

¼ CUP HONEY

2 TABLESPOONS WHOLE-GRAIN
MUSTARD

3 TABLESPOONS APPLE
CIDER VINEGAR

1 TEASPOON KOSHER SALT

½ TEASPOON BLACK PEPPER

⅓ CUP OLIVE OIL

4. To prepare the vinaigrette, place all of the ingredients, except for the oil, in a small mixing bowl and whisk to combine. Add the oil in a slow stream and whisk until emulsified.

5. Place the beets, except for the red variety, in a salad bowl. Add the radishes, radish greens, and apples and toss to combine. Add half of the vinaigrette, season with salt and pepper, and toss to evenly coat.

6. Spread the mousse on the serving dishes. Place salad on top, sprinkle the red beets over the salad, drizzle the remaining vinaigrette on top, and garnish each portion with a piece of honeycomb.

Late Summer Salad with Wild Mushrooms, Parmesan & Pine Nuts

YIELD: **4 SERVINGS**

ACTIVE TIME: **25 MINUTES**

TOTAL TIME: **35 MINUTES**

INGREDIENTS

¼ CUP OLIVE OIL, PLUS MORE AS NEEDED

½ LB. MUSHROOMS, SLICED

SALT, TO TASTE

1 RED ONION, DICED

1 GARLIC CLOVE, MINCED

¼ CUP BALSAMIC VINEGAR

¼ CUP PINE NUTS

MESCLUN SALAD GREENS, FOR SERVING

¼ CUP GRATED PARMESAN CHEESE

FRESH DILL, FINELY CHOPPED, TO TASTE

DIRECTIONS

1. Place a few tablespoons of oil in a large skillet and warm it over medium-high heat. When the oil starts to shimmer, add the mushrooms, making sure not to crowd the pan. Sprinkle a pinch of salt over the mushrooms as they cook but leave them undisturbed until they release their liquid and begin to brown. Gently turn them over to sear the other side. When well browned on both sides, transfer the mushrooms to a small bowl.

2. Add the onion, garlic, and, if the pan looks dry, a splash of olive oil. Sauté over medium heat until the onion starts to soften, about 5 minutes. Remove the pan from heat and deglaze it with the balsamic vinegar, scraping up any browned bits on the bottom. Let the pan cool to room temperature.

3. Place the pine nuts in a small skillet and toast over medium heat for a few minutes, being careful not to burn them. Transfer the pine nuts to a small bowl and let cool.

4. Place the cooled onion mixture in a bowl and add the ¼ cup olive oil. Whisk until combined and season to taste.

5. Arrange the greens on plates and top each portion with the mushrooms, pine nuts, and a light sprinkling of Parmesan and dill. Top with the dressed onion mixture and serve.

Red & Green Cabbage Salad with Ginger & Tahini Dressing

YIELD: **2 SERVINGS**

ACTIVE TIME: **15 MINUTES**

TOTAL TIME: **15 MINUTES**

INGREDIENTS

FOR THE SALAD

2 CUPS SHREDDED GREEN CABBAGE

2 CUPS SHREDDED RED CABBAGE

3 TABLESPOONS CHOPPED PEANUTS

3 SCALLIONS, TRIMMED AND CHOPPED

½ CUP FINELY CHOPPED FRESH CILANTRO OR PARSLEY

FOR THE DRESSING

¼ CUP TAHINI

2 TABLESPOONS FRESH LEMON JUICE

2 GARLIC CLOVES, MINCED

1 TEASPOON REAL MAPLE SYRUP

½-INCH PIECE OF FRESH GINGER, PEELED AND GRATED

1 TEASPOON RICE VINEGAR

1 TEASPOON TOASTED SESAME OIL

½ CUP OLIVE OIL

DIRECTIONS

1. To prepare the salad, place all of the ingredients in a salad bowl and toss to combine.

2. To prepare the dressing, place all of the ingredients in a bowl and whisk vigorously until emulsified.

3. Add about ¼ cup of the dressing to the salad and toss to coat. Taste and add more dressing if desired.

Chili-Dusted Cauliflower & Chickpea Salad

YIELD: **4 SERVINGS**

ACTIVE TIME: **25 MINUTES**

TOTAL TIME: **45 MINUTES**

INGREDIENTS

FOR THE SALAD

1 (14 OZ.) CAN OF CHICKPEAS, DRAINED AND RINSED

3 CUPS CAULIFLOWER FLORETS

3 GARLIC CLOVES, SLICED THIN

1 SHALLOT, SLICED THIN

⅓ CUP OLIVE OIL

½ TEASPOON CHILI POWDER

½ TEASPOON CHIPOTLE CHILI POWDER

½ TEASPOON BLACK PEPPER

½ TEASPOON ONION POWDER

½ TEASPOON GARLIC POWDER

¼ TEASPOON PAPRIKA

1 TABLESPOON KOSHER SALT

Continued...

DIRECTIONS

1. Preheat the oven to 400°F. To prepare the salad, place all of the ingredients in a mixing bowl and toss to coat. Place the mixture in a 9 x 13–inch baking pan, place the pan in the oven, and roast until the cauliflower is slightly charred and still crunchy, about 30 minutes. Remove from the oven and let the mixture cool slightly.

2. To prepare the dressing, place all of the ingredients in a food processor and blitz until combined. Place the cooked cauliflower-and-chickpea mixture in the bowl, toss to coat, and serve.

FOR THE DRESSING

2 SCALLIONS, TRIMMED AND
SLICED THIN

2 FRESNO CHILI PEPPERS,
STEMMED, SEEDS AND RIBS
REMOVED, AND SLICED THIN

3 TABLESPOONS SUGAR

¼ CUP RED WINE VINEGAR

½ TEASPOON CHILI POWDER

½ TEASPOON CHIPOTLE
CHILI POWDER

½ TEASPOON BLACK PEPPER

½ TEASPOON ONION POWDER

½ TEASPOON GARLIC POWDER

¼ TEASPOON PAPRIKA

½ TABLESPOON KOSHER SALT

Coconut & Cucumber Salad

INGREDIENTS

5 LARGE CUCUMBERS, PEELED, HALVED LENGTHWISE, AND SEEDED

½ CUP SHREDDED UNSWEETENED COCONUT

ZEST AND JUICE OF 2 LIMES

¼ CUP COCONUT MILK

1 TEASPOON CHILI GARLIC SAUCE, PLUS MORE AS NEEDED

½-INCH PIECE OF FRESH GINGER, PEELED AND GRATED

1 TEASPOON SUGAR

1 TEASPOON CUMIN

1 TEASPOON KOSHER SALT, PLUS MORE TO TASTE

½ CUP ROASTED PEANUTS, CHOPPED, FOR SERVING

6 SCALLIONS, TRIMMED AND SLICED THIN, FOR SERVING

DIRECTIONS

1. Quarter each cucumber half and then cut the quarters into long, ⅛-inch-wide strips. Place the strips on paper towels to drain.

2. Place the coconut, lime juice, coconut milk, chili garlic sauce, ginger, sugar, cumin, and salt in a food processor and blitz until smooth.

3. Place the cucumbers in a large serving bowl. Add the coconut mixture and toss to coat.

4. Sprinkle the lime zest, peanuts, and scallions on top of the dressed cucumbers, season to taste, and serve immediately.

Vegetarian Rice Bowl with Benihana's Ginger Dressing

YIELD: **4 SERVINGS**

ACTIVE TIME: **30 MINUTES**

TOTAL TIME: **45 MINUTES**

INGREDIENTS

FOR THE SALAD

1 TABLESPOON OLIVE OIL

1 LB. EXTRA-FIRM TOFU, DRAINED AND CHOPPED

2 CUPS COOKED WHITE RICE, AT ROOM TEMPERATURE

2 CARROTS, PEELED AND GRATED

1 CUP BROCCOLI SPROUTS

1 CUP CORN KERNELS

1 CUP COOKED EDAMAME

FLESH OF 2 AVOCADOS, SLICED THIN

SALT, TO TASTE

SESAME SEEDS, FOR GARNISH

Continued...

DIRECTIONS

1. To begin preparations for the salad, place the oil in a large skillet and warm over medium-high heat. When the oil starts to shimmer, add the tofu and cook until it is browned all over, turning the pieces as necessary, about 10 minutes.

2. To prepare the dressing, place all of the ingredients in a food processor and blitz until smooth.

3. Divide the rice between four bowls. Arrange the tofu, carrots, broccoli sprouts, corn, edamame, and avocados on top of each portion. Season with salt, drizzle the dressing over the top, garnish with the sesame seeds, and serve.

FOR THE DRESSING

¼ CUP CHOPPED WHITE ONION

¼ CUP PEANUT OIL

1 TABLESPOON RICE VINEGAR

1-INCH PIECE OF FRESH GINGER,
PEELED AND MINCED

1 TABLESPOON MINCED CELERY

1 TABLESPOON SOY SAUCE

1 TEASPOON TOMATO PASTE

1½ TEASPOONS SUGAR

1 TEASPOON FRESH LEMON JUICE

½ TEASPOON KOSHER SALT

BLACK PEPPER, TO TASTE

CHAPTER 3

SOUPS &

STEWS

---

*Comforting, easy to prepare, and able to accommodate
an incredible amount of contrasting flavors, these preparations are
some of the most exciting in the entire book. Containing a balance of low-
and-slow favorites and ready-in-a-flash preparations, the majority of the
soups in this section will make for a perfect light lunch or first course,
but some are hearty enough to serve as the main event. Whichever
one you choose, you can be sure it will soothe your mind and
body, no matter what shape your day has taken.*

Roasted Corn & Red Pepper Soup

YIELD: **4 SERVINGS**

ACTIVE TIME: **30 MINUTES**

TOTAL TIME: **1 HOUR AND 30 MINUTES**

INGREDIENTS

3 CUPS FRESH CORN KERNELS

2 TABLESPOONS OLIVE OIL

SALT AND PEPPER, TO TASTE

3 RED PEPPERS

4 TABLESPOONS UNSALTED BUTTER

½ CUP HEAVY CREAM

½ CUP MILK

DIRECTIONS

1. Preheat the oven to 375°F. Place the corn in a single layer on a large baking sheet and drizzle the oil over it. Season with salt, place the corn in the oven, and roast until it starts to darken and caramelize, 12 to 18 minutes. Remove from the oven and raise the temperature to 425°F.

2. Place the peppers on another baking sheet and place them in the oven. Cook, while turning occasionally, until the skins are blistered all over, about 30 minutes. Remove the peppers from the oven and let them cool. When cool enough to handle, remove the stems, skins, and seeds and discard. Set the peppers aside.

3. Place the corn, peppers, butter, cream, and milk in a saucepan and bring to a simmer over medium heat, stirring frequently. Simmer the soup for 20 minutes, making sure that it does not come to a boil. After simmering for 20 minutes, remove the pan from heat and let the soup cool for 10 minutes.

4. Transfer the soup to a blender and puree until smooth. If the soup has cooled too much, return it to the saucepan and cook until warmed through. If not, ladle into warmed bowls and serve.

Miso Ramen with Spicy Bean Sprout Salad

YIELD: **4 SERVINGS**

ACTIVE TIME: **20 MINUTES**

TOTAL TIME: **45 MINUTES**

INGREDIENTS

FOR THE SALAD

¾ LB. BEAN SPROUTS

1 TABLESPOON SESAME SEEDS

2 SCALLIONS, TRIMMED AND SLICED THIN

2 TABLESPOONS SESAME OIL

2 TEASPOONS SOY SAUCE

⅛ TEASPOON RED PEPPER FLAKES

PINCH OF GROUND GINGER

ZEST OF 1 ORANGE

Continued...

DIRECTIONS

1. To prepare the salad, bring water to a boil in a small saucepan. Add the bean sprouts and cook for 2 minutes. Drain and let cool. Place the remaining ingredients in a salad bowl and stir to combine. Add the cooled bean sprouts, gently stir to incorporate, and set the salad aside.

2. To begin preparations for the ramen, place the sesame seeds in a dry skillet and toast over medium heat until browned, about 2 minutes. Remove the sesame seeds from the pan and use a mortar and pestle to grind them into a paste, adding water as needed.

3. Place the sesame oil in a large saucepan and warm over medium heat. When the oil starts to shimmer, add the garlic, ginger, and shallots and sauté until fragrant, about 2 minutes.

4. Raise the heat to medium-high and stir in the chili garlic sauce, miso, toasted sesame paste, sugar, sake, and stock. Bring to a boil, reduce heat so that the soup simmers, and season with salt and pepper. Simmer for about 5 minutes and remove from heat.

5. While the soup is simmering, cook the noodles according to the manufacturer's instructions. Drain the noodles and place them in warmed bowls. Pour the soup over the noodles and top each portion with the bean sprout salad.

TIP: If you're looking to add some substance to this ramen, top each portion with a poached egg. If you want to make it even heartier, thinly sliced chicken or beef will work wonderfully with the broth.

FOR THE RAMEN

¼ CUP SESAME SEEDS

2 TABLESPOONS SESAME OIL

4 GARLIC CLOVES, MINCED

2-INCH PIECE OF FRESH GINGER,
PEELED AND MINCED

2 SHALLOTS, MINCED

2 TEASPOONS CHILI GARLIC SAUCE

6 TABLESPOONS WHITE
MISO PASTE

2 TABLESPOONS SUGAR

2 TABLESPOONS SAKE

8 CUPS VEGETABLE STOCK
(SEE PAGE 140)

SALT AND PEPPER, TO TASTE

NOODLES FROM 2 PACKAGES
OF RAMEN

PICKLED RED GINGER,
FOR GARNISH

SPICED CRÈME FRAÎCHE

Place 1 cup crème fraîche, ½ teaspoon cinnamon, ⅛ teaspoon freshly grated nutmeg, ⅛ teaspoon ground cloves, and 1 tablespoon real maple syrup in a bowl and stir to combine.

Pumpkin Bisque

INGREDIENTS

1 LONG ISLAND CHEESE PUMPKIN

6 TABLESPOONS UNSALTED BUTTER

2 YELLOW ONIONS, SLICED

2 GARLIC CLOVES, MINCED

4 CUPS MILK

1 CUP HEAVY CREAM

1 TABLESPOON KOSHER SALT, PLUS ½ TEASPOON

2 TABLESPOONS BROWN SUGAR

1 TABLESPOON OLIVE OIL

¼ TEASPOON BLACK PEPPER

¼ TEASPOON PAPRIKA

SPICED CRÈME FRAÎCHE (SEE SIDEBAR)

REAL MAPLE SYRUP, FOR GARNISH

DIRECTIONS

1. Preheat the oven to 350°F. Cut the pumpkin in half lengthwise, remove the seeds, and reserve them. Place the halves of pumpkin on an aluminum foil–lined baking sheet, cut side down. Place the pumpkin in the oven and roast until the flesh is tender, about 40 minutes. Remove from the oven, taking care not to spill any of the juices, and let the pumpkin cool. Leave the oven on.

2. Place the butter in a saucepan and melt it over medium-high heat. Add the onions and garlic and sauté until the onions are translucent, about 3 minutes. Stir in the milk, cream, sugar, and tablespoon of salt and reduce the heat to medium. Scoop the pumpkin's flesh into the pan, bring the soup to a boil, and then reduce the heat so that it simmers. Cook, while stirring occasionally, for 20 minutes.

3. While the soup is simmering, run the reserved pumpkin seeds under water to remove any pulp. Pat them dry, place them on a baking sheet, drizzle the olive oil over the top, and sprinkle them with the remaining salt, the pepper, and paprika. Place in the oven and toast until light brown and crispy, 6 to 8 minutes. Remove from the oven and set aside.

4. Working in batches, transfer the soup to a blender and puree until smooth. Season to taste, ladle into bowls, and top each portion with a dollop of the Spiced Crème Fraîche, the toasted pumpkin seeds, and a drizzle of maple syrup.

Creamy Curry Kuri Soup

INGREDIENTS

1 LARGE KURI SQUASH,
QUARTERED AND SEEDED

1 LARGE ONION, SLICED

2 TABLESPOONS OLIVE OIL

SALT AND PEPPER, TO TASTE

2 TABLESPOONS CURRY POWDER

4 TABLESPOONS UNSALTED BUTTER

1 CUP HEAVY CREAM

1 CUP WHOLE MILK

2 SPRIGS OF FRESH ROSEMARY

2 SPRIGS OF FRESH THYME

DIRECTIONS

1. Preheat the oven to 400°F. Place the squash and onion in a baking dish, drizzle the olive oil over the top, and season with salt. Place the dish in the oven and roast until the onion has browned, 15 to 25 minutes. Remove the dish from the oven, transfer the onion to a bowl, return the squash to the oven, and roast until the flesh is tender, another 20 to 35 minutes. Remove the squash from the oven and let it cool.

2. When the squash is cool enough to handle, scoop out the seeds. Scrape the flesh into the bowl containing the onion and stir to combine. Place the squash, onion, and remaining ingredients in a large saucepan and bring to a boil over medium-high heat. Reduce heat to low and let the mixture simmer for 15 to 20 minutes, stirring occasionally.

3. Remove the sprigs of thyme and rosemary. Transfer the soup to a blender and puree until desired texture is achieved. Season with salt and pepper and ladle the soup into warmed bowls.

NOTE: The toasted squash seeds will make for a lovely garnish for this soup. To do this, wash the seeds to remove any pulp and then pat them dry. Transfer them to a baking sheet, drizzle with olive oil, sprinkle with salt, and place the sheet in the oven. Bake for 5 minutes, remove them from the oven, and turn them over. Return to the oven and bake for another 5 minutes, until golden brown.

VEGETABLE STOCK

Place 2 tablespoons olive oil, 2 trimmed and well rinsed leeks, 2 peeled and sliced carrots, 2 celery stalks, 2 sliced onions, and 3 unpeeled, smashed garlic cloves in a large stockpot and cook over low heat until the liquid the vegetables release has evaporated. Add 2 sprigs of fresh parsley and thyme, 1 bay leaf, 8 cups water, ½ teaspoon black peppercorns, and salt to taste. Raise the heat to high and bring the stock to a boil. Reduce heat so that the stock simmers and cook for 2 hours, skimming to remove any impurities that float to the surface. Strain the stock through a fine sieve, let the stock cool slightly, and place it in the refrigerator, uncovered, to chill. Remove the fat layer and cover. The stock will keep in the refrigerator for 3 to 5 days, and in the freezer for up to 3 months.

YIELD: **4 SERVINGS**

ACTIVE TIME: **20 MINUTES**

TOTAL TIME: **45 MINUTES**

Artichoke Soup with Fennel Seed Yogurt

INGREDIENTS

FOR THE SOUP

6 ARTICHOKES

1 TABLESPOON OLIVE OIL

1 TABLESPOON UNSALTED BUTTER

1 GARLIC CLOVE, MINCED

1 YELLOW ONION, CHOPPED

1 CUP RIESLING

1 TABLESPOON FINELY CHOPPED
FRESH THYME

4 CUPS HEAVY CREAM

1 CUP VEGETABLE STOCK
(SEE SIDEBAR)

SALT AND PEPPER, TO TASTE

FRESH DILL, FINELY CHOPPED,
FOR GARNISH

FOR THE YOGURT

1 CUP PLAIN GREEK YOGURT

2 TABLESPOONS PERNOD

1 TEASPOON GROUND FENNEL

DIRECTIONS

1. To begin preparations for the soup, peel the artichokes, remove the hearts, and slice them thin.

2. Place the oil and butter in a medium saucepan and warm over medium heat. When the butter has melted, add the artichoke hearts, garlic, and onion and sauté for 10 minutes.

3. Stir in the Riesling and thyme and cook until the wine has reduced by half. Add the heavy cream and the stock and simmer for 10 minutes.

4. While the soup is simmering, prepare the yogurt. Place all of the ingredients in a mixing bowl, stir to combine, and refrigerate until ready to use.

5. Transfer the soup to a food processor or blender, puree until smooth, and strain through a fine sieve. Season with salt and pepper, ladle into warmed bowls, top each portion with some of the fennel seed yogurt, and garnish with dill.

Carrot & Ginger Soup with Turmeric Cream

INGREDIENTS

FOR THE SOUP

4 TABLESPOONS UNSALTED BUTTER

2 YELLOW ONIONS, CHOPPED

6 CARROTS, PEELED AND CHOPPED

4-INCH PIECE OF FRESH GINGER, PEELED AND MINCED

ZEST AND JUICE OF 2 ORANGES

1 CUP WHITE WINE

8 CUPS VEGETABLE STOCK (SEE PAGE 140), PLUS MORE AS NEEDED

SALT AND PEPPER, TO TASTE

FRESH DILL, FINELY CHOPPED, FOR GARNISH

FOR THE TURMERIC CREAM

½ CUP HEAVY CREAM

½ TEASPOON TURMERIC

PINCH OF KOSHER SALT

DIRECTIONS

1. To begin preparations for the soup, place the butter in a medium saucepan and melt it over medium heat. Add the onions and sauté until they start to soften, about 5 minutes.

2. Add the carrots, ginger, and orange zest. Sauté until the carrots start to soften, about 5 minutes, stir in the orange juice and white wine, and cook until they have evaporated, scraping up the browned bits from the bottom of the pan. Add the stock, bring to a boil, and season the soup with salt and pepper. Reduce the heat so that the soup simmers and cook until the vegetables are tender, 10 to 15 minutes.

3. Transfer the soup to a food processor or blender, puree until smooth, and strain through a fine sieve. Return the soup to a clean saucepan, taste, and adjust the seasoning if needed. Add more stock if the consistency is too thick. Return the soup to a gentle simmer and then remove the pan from heat.

4. To prepare the turmeric cream, place the cream in a bowl and beat with a handheld mixer fitted with the whisk attachment, at high speed, until soft peaks start to form. Add the turmeric, season with salt, and stir to incorporate.

5. Ladle the soup into warm bowls, top each portion with a dollop of the turmeric cream, and garnish with the dill.

YIELD: **6 SERVINGS**

ACTIVE TIME: **30 MINUTES**

TOTAL TIME: **1 HOUR**

Creamy Leek Soup

INGREDIENTS

FOR THE SOUP

4 TABLESPOONS UNSALTED BUTTER

2 TABLESPOONS OLIVE OIL

3 LARGE LEEKS, TRIMMED, RINSED WELL, AND SLICED THIN

½ LB. CASHEL BLUE CHEESE

2 TABLESPOONS ALL-PURPOSE FLOUR

1 TABLESPOON WHOLE-GRAIN MUSTARD, PLUS MORE FOR GARNISH

6 CUPS VEGETABLE STOCK (SEE PAGE 140)

BLACK PEPPER, TO TASTE

FRESH CHIVES, FINELY CHOPPED, FOR GARNISH

FOR THE FRITTERS

VEGETABLE OIL, AS NEEDED

6 OZ. CASHEL BLUE CHEESE

3 EGGS

¼ CUP ALL-PURPOSE FLOUR

1 CUP PANKO, FINELY GROUND

DIRECTIONS

1. To begin preparations for the soup, place the butter and oil in a large saucepan and warm over low heat. When the butter has melted, add the leeks and sauté until they start to soften, about 5 minutes.

2. Break the Cashel blue into small pieces and add them to the saucepan. Cook, while stirring, until the cheese has melted. Add the flour and cook for 2 minutes, stirring constantly, then incorporate the mustard.

3. Slowly add the stock, stirring to prevent any lumps from forming. Bring the soup to a boil, reduce the heat so that it simmers, and cook for 10 minutes.

4. While the soup is simmering, prepare the fritters. Add oil to a Dutch oven until it is 2 inches deep and warm it to 350°F. Cut the blue cheese into 12 cubes. Place the eggs in a bowl and beat them with a fork. Place the flour and panko in separate bowls. Dredge the cheese in the flour and shake to remove any excess. Dredge the cheese in the egg wash until evenly coated. Remove from the egg wash, shake to remove any excess, and dredge in the panko until coated. Place the breaded cheese in the hot oil and fry until golden brown. Use a slotted spoon to remove the fritters from the oil, set on paper towels to drain, and season with salt.

5. Season the soup with pepper and ladle it into warmed bowls. Garnish with chives and additional mustard and serve with the blue cheese fritters.

YIELD: **4 SERVINGS**

ACTIVE TIME: **45 MINUTES**

TOTAL TIME: **24 HOURS**

Clarified Tomato Soup

INGREDIENTS

FOR THE SOUP

10 LARGE RIPE TOMATOES, CHOPPED

1 TEASPOON FINELY CHOPPED FRESH THYME

1 STAR ANISE POD

1 TABLESPOON RICE

2 CUPS HEAVY CREAM

SALT AND PEPPER, TO TASTE

FOR THE CONFIT CHERRY TOMATOES

12 CHERRY TOMATOES

1 GARLIC CLOVE, SLICED VERY THIN

ZEST OF 1 LEMON

1 TABLESPOON OLIVE OIL

SALT AND PEPPER, TO TASTE

DIRECTIONS

1. To begin preparations for the soup, place the tomatoes in a food processor and puree for 5 minutes. Working over a large bowl, strain the puree through cheesecloth overnight.

2. Place the strained tomato water, thyme, star anise pod, and rice in a medium saucepan and cook over medium heat until the liquid has reduced by half. Add the cream and gently simmer for 30 minutes.

3. While the soup is simmering, preheat the oven to 300°F and prepare the confit cherry tomatoes. Place the tomatoes on a baking sheet and sprinkle the garlic and lemon zest over them. Drizzle with olive oil and season with salt and pepper. Place in oven and roast for 15 minutes, until the tomatoes' skins are blistered and they start to collapse. Remove and let cool.

4. Remove the star anise pod from the soup and discard. Transfer the soup to a blender and puree until smooth and creamy. Strain through a fine sieve, return it to the pan, season with salt and pepper, and bring to a simmer.

5. Ladle the soup into bowls and serve with the confit cherry tomatoes on the side.

NOTE: It is very important to choose ripe tomatoes for this dish. If they are even slightly off, this soup can get very acidic.

YIELD: **4 SERVINGS**

ACTIVE TIME: **20 MINUTES**

TOTAL TIME: **45 MINUTES**

Spicy Carrot Soup

INGREDIENTS

1 TABLESPOON OLIVE OIL

1 ONION, CHOPPED

1 GARLIC CLOVE, MINCED

2 TABLESPOONS CURRY POWDER

6 CUPS VEGETABLE STOCK
(SEE PAGE 140)

1 BIRD'S EYE CHILI PEPPER,
STEMMED, SEEDS AND RIBS
REMOVED, AND SLICED

ZEST AND JUICE OF 1 LIME

2 TABLESPOONS SOY SAUCE

¼ CUP JAGGERY

2 MAKRUT LIME LEAVES

1 CARROT, PEELED AND JULIENNED

2 CUPS SPINACH

¾ LB. EXTRA-FIRM TOFU, DRAINED
AND CHOPPED

SALT AND PEPPER, TO TASTE

DIRECTIONS

1. Place the oil in a large saucepan and warm it over medium heat. When the oil starts to shimmer, add the onion, garlic, and curry powder and sauté until the onion starts to soften, about 5 minutes.

2. Add the stock, chili pepper, lime zest and juice, soy sauce, jaggery, and lime leaves. Bring the soup to a boil, reduce the heat so that it simmers, and cook for 10 minutes.

3. Add the carrot and continue to simmer for 5 minutes. Stir in the spinach and tofu just prior to serving. Season the soup with salt and pepper and ladle into warmed bowls.

Cream of Mushroom

INGREDIENTS

4 TABLESPOONS UNSALTED BUTTER

1 ONION, CHOPPED

2 GARLIC CLOVES, CHOPPED

⅓ CUP MADEIRA

¾ LB. WILD MUSHROOMS

4 CUPS VEGETABLE STOCK
(SEE PAGE 140)

1½ CUPS FUSILLI PASTA

1 CUP HEAVY CREAM

SALT AND PEPPER, TO TASTE

FRESH PARSLEY, FINELY CHOPPED,
FOR GARNISH

DIRECTIONS

1. Place the butter in a large saucepan and melt it over medium heat. Add the onion and garlic and sauté until the onion starts to soften, about 5 minutes.

2. Stir in the Madeira and cook until it has evaporated, about 5 minutes. Add the mushrooms and cook until they have released all of their liquid and start to brown, about 10 minutes.

3. Add the stock and bring the soup to a boil. Reduce the heat so that it simmers and cook for 10 minutes.

4. Transfer the soup to a blender, puree until smooth and creamy, and then strain through a fine sieve.

5. Return the soup to a clean saucepan and bring it to a simmer. Add the fusilli and cook until it is tender, about 8 minutes.

6. Add the heavy cream and simmer for 2 minutes while stirring constantly. Season with salt and pepper, ladle the soup into warmed bowls, and garnish with parsley.

NOTE: Fusilli is recommended because it has the ideal texture for this soup. But feel free to substitute your favorite pasta, or whatever's in the cupboard.

LAKSA CURRY PASTE

Place 2 teaspoons coriander seeds and ½ teaspoon fennel seeds in a dry skillet and toast until fragrant, about 2 minutes, stirring to make sure they don't burn. Place the seeds in a food processor along with 1 teaspoon turmeric, 1 tablespoon minced fresh ginger, 1 seeded and chopped green chili pepper, ½ teaspoon cayenne pepper, 1 lemongrass stalk, 2 garlic cloves, 2 tablespoons cashews, ½ cup finely chopped fresh cilantro, 1 teaspoon fresh lime juice, and 2 tablespoons water. Blitz until the mixture is a paste and season with salt and pepper.

YIELD: **4 SERVINGS**

ACTIVE TIME: **20 MINUTES**

TOTAL TIME: **45 MINUTES**

Laksa Soup

INGREDIENTS

1 TABLESPOON OLIVE OIL

LAKSA CURRY PASTE (SEE SIDEBAR)

2 CUPS SLICED SHIITAKE
MUSHROOMS

2 CARROTS, PEELED AND SLICED

¼ CUP CHOPPED RED BELL PEPPERS

¼ CUP CHOPPED GREEN
BELL PEPPERS

¼ CUP CHOPPED ZUCCHINI

¼ CUP CHOPPED YELLOW SQUASH

4 CUPS VEGETABLE STOCK
(SEE PAGE 140)

1 (14 OZ.) CAN OF COCONUT MILK

½ LB. RICE NOODLES

1 CUP CHOPPED KALE

½ LB. EXTRA-FIRM TOFU, CHOPPED

1 TABLESPOON SOY SAUCE

1 TABLESPOON FRESH LIME JUICE

1 TEASPOON SUGAR

SALT AND PEPPER, TO TASTE

2 BIRD'S EYE CHILI PEPPERS,
STEMMED, SEEDS AND RIBS
REMOVED, AND SLICED,
FOR GARNISH

FRESH CILANTRO, FINELY
CHOPPED, FOR GARNISH

DIRECTIONS

1. Place the oil in a large saucepan and warm over medium heat. When the oil starts to shimmer, add the Laksa Curry Paste and cook for 3 minutes, stirring constantly.

2. Add the mushrooms and sauté for 2 minutes. Add the carrots, bell peppers, zucchini, and yellow squash and sauté until they start to soften, about 5 minutes.

3. Add the stock and coconut milk and bring the soup to a boil. Reduce the heat so that the soup simmers, stir in the noodles, and cook for 10 minutes.

4. Fold in the kale and tofu, let the soup simmer for another 2 minutes, and then stir in the soy sauce, lime juice, and sugar. Season with salt and pepper, ladle the soup into warmed bowls, and garnish with the chilies and cilantro.

Crispy Cauliflower Soup

INGREDIENTS

FOR THE SOUP

2 TABLESPOONS OLIVE OIL

1 ONION, CHOPPED

2 GARLIC CLOVES, MINCED

1 HEAD OF CAULIFLOWER, TRIMMED AND CHOPPED

4 CUPS VEGETABLE STOCK (SEE PAGE 140)

¾ CUP QUINOA, RINSED

2 TABLESPOONS FINELY CHOPPED FRESH THYME

½ CUP HEAVY CREAM

SALT AND PEPPER, TO TASTE

FRESH CHIVES, FINELY CHOPPED, FOR GARNISH

FOR THE CRISPY CAULIFLOWER

VEGETABLE OIL, AS NEEDED

4 CUPS WATER

SALT AND PEPPER, TO TASTE

12 SMALL CAULIFLOWER FLORETS

¾ CUP ALL-PURPOSE FLOUR

¼ CUP CORNSTARCH

½ TEASPOON BAKING POWDER

1 CUP SODA WATER

DIRECTIONS

1. To begin preparations for the soup, place the oil in a large saucepan and warm it over medium heat. When the oil starts to shimmer, add the onion and sauté until it starts to soften, about 5 minutes.

2. Add the garlic and sauté until fragrant, about 1 minute. Add the cauliflower, stock, quinoa, and thyme and bring the soup to a boil. Reduce heat so that it simmers, cover the pan, and cook until the cauliflower and quinoa are tender, about 15 minutes.

3. While the soup is simmering, begin preparations for the crispy cauliflower. Add oil to a Dutch oven until it is 2 inches deep and warm it to 350°F. Prepare an ice water bath in a mixing bowl. Place the water in a small saucepan and bring to a boil. Add salt and the cauliflower to the boiling water, cook for 3 minutes, and transfer it to the ice water bath. When the cauliflower is cool, set it on paper towels to drain.

4. Sift ½ cup of the flour, the cornstarch, and baking powder into a mixing bowl. Add the soda water and whisk until smooth. Place the remaining flour and the cauliflower in a small bowl and toss until the florets are evenly coated.

5. Dip each piece of cauliflower into the batter and then gently drop them into the oil. Fry until golden brown, remove with a slotted spoon, and set on a paper towel–lined plate to drain. Season with salt and pepper and let cool slightly.

6. Stir the heavy cream into the soup, season with salt and pepper, and ladle into warmed bowls. Top each portion with the crispy cauliflower and chives.

Minestrone

INGREDIENTS

2 TABLESPOONS OLIVE OIL

1 GARLIC CLOVE, MINCED

2 ONIONS, MINCED

2 CARROTS, PEELED AND MINCED

1 LEEK, WHITE PART ONLY, RINSED WELL AND MINCED

2 YELLOW BELL PEPPERS, STEMMED, SEEDS AND RIBS REMOVED, AND MINCED

2 RED BELL PEPPERS, STEMMED, SEEDS AND RIBS REMOVED, AND MINCED

2 ZUCCHINI, MINCED

8 CHERRY TOMATOES, CHOPPED

6 CUPS TOMATO JUICE

½ TEASPOON FINELY CHOPPED FRESH THYME

½ TEASPOON FINELY CHOPPED FRESH ROSEMARY

SALT AND PEPPER, TO TASTE

PARMESAN CHEESE, SHAVED, FOR GARNISH

DIRECTIONS

1. Place the oil in a large saucepan and warm it over medium heat. When the oil starts to shimmer, add the garlic, onions, carrots, and leek and sauté until the vegetables start to soften, about 5 minutes.

2. Add the peppers, cook for 5 minutes, and then stir in the zucchini and cherry tomatoes. Cook for 3 minutes, add the tomato juice, thyme, and rosemary, and bring the soup to a boil.

3. Reduce the heat so that the soup simmers and cook until the vegetables are tender, about 20 minutes. Season with salt and pepper, ladle into warmed bowls, and garnish with the Parmesan.

Go for the Green Stew

INGREDIENTS

1 TABLESPOON OLIVE OIL

1 ONION, CHOPPED

2 GARLIC CLOVES, MINCED

1 CELERY STALK, MINCED

1 GREEN BELL PEPPER, STEMMED,
SEEDS AND RIBS REMOVED,
AND CHOPPED

¼ HEAD OF GREEN CABBAGE,
CORED AND SLICED THIN

½ TEASPOON FINELY CHOPPED
FRESH OREGANO

½ TEASPOON FINELY CHOPPED
FRESH THYME

1 BAY LEAF

6 CUPS VEGETABLE STOCK
(SEE PAGE 140)

2 CUPS SHREDDED COLLARD
GREENS

2 CUPS SHREDDED BABY SPINACH

1 BUNCH OF WATERCRESS

¾ LB. TOFU, DRAINED AND
CHOPPED INTO ¼-INCH PIECES

¼ CUP FINELY CHOPPED FRESH
PARSLEY

½ TEASPOON ALLSPICE

PINCH OF CAYENNE PEPPER

SALT AND PEPPER, TO TASTE

DIRECTIONS

1. Place the olive oil in a large saucepan and warm it over medium heat. When the oil starts to shimmer, add the onion, garlic, celery, and bell pepper and sauté until the onion and celery start to soften, about 5 minutes.

2. Stir in the cabbage, oregano, thyme, and bay leaf, cook for 5 minutes, and then add the stock. Bring the stew to a boil, reduce heat so that it simmers, and cook for 5 minutes.

3. Stir in the collard greens and cook for 5 minutes. Add the spinach, watercress, and tofu and cook for 2 minutes before stirring in the parsley, allspice, and cayenne. Season with salt and pepper, simmer for 2 more minutes, and ladle into warmed bowls.

CHICKEN STOCK

Place 3 lbs. rinsed chicken bones in a large stockpot, cover them with water, and bring to a boil. Add 1 chopped onion, 2 chopped carrots, 3 chopped celery stalks, 3 unpeeled, smashed garlic cloves, 3 sprigs of fresh thyme, 1 teaspoon black peppercorns, 1 bay leaf, season the stock with salt, and reduce the heat so that the stock simmers. Cook for 2 hours, skimming to remove any impurities that float to the surface. Strain the stock through a fine sieve, let the stock cool slightly, and place it in the refrigerator, uncovered, to chill. Remove the fat layer and cover. The stock will keep in the refrigerator for 3 to 5 days, and in the freezer for up to 3 months.

Split Pea Soup with Smoked Ham

YIELD: **4 SERVINGS**

ACTIVE TIME: **30 MINUTES**

TOTAL TIME: **2 HOURS**

INGREDIENTS

2 TABLESPOONS UNSALTED BUTTER

1 ONION, MINCED

1 CARROT, PEELED AND MINCED

1 CELERY STALK, MINCED

5 CUPS CHICKEN STOCK
(SEE SIDEBAR)

1 CUP SPLIT PEAS

½ LB. SMOKED HAM, CHOPPED

2 TABLESPOONS FINELY CHOPPED
FRESH PARSLEY, PLUS MORE
FOR GARNISH

1 BAY LEAF

1 TEASPOON FINELY CHOPPED
FRESH THYME

SALT AND PEPPER, TO TASTE

LEMON WEDGES, FOR SERVING

DIRECTIONS

1. Place the butter in a large saucepan and melt it over medium heat. Add the onion, carrot, and celery and sauté until they have softened, about 5 minutes.

2. Add the stock, split peas, ham, parsley, bay leaf, and thyme. Bring the soup to a boil, reduce the heat to medium-low, and simmer the soup, stirring occasionally, until the peas are al dente, about 1 hour.

3. Remove the bay leaf and discard it. Season the soup with salt and pepper and ladle it into warmed bowls. Garnish with additional parsley and serve with lemon wedges.

YIELD: **4 SERVINGS**

ACTIVE TIME: **30 MINUTES**

TOTAL TIME: **24 HOURS**

Chamin

INGREDIENTS

1½ TABLESPOONS OLIVE OIL

1 SMALL ONION, CHOPPED

5 GARLIC CLOVES, MINCED

¾ CUP CHOPPED PARSNIP

2 CARROTS, PEELED AND SLICED

1 TEASPOON CUMIN

¼ TEASPOON TURMERIC

1½-INCH PIECE OF FRESH GINGER,
PEELED AND MINCED

½ LB. BEEF BRISKET, TRIMMED
AND CHOPPED

4 OZ. LAMB SHOULDER, TRIMMED
AND CHOPPED

4 CUPS BEEF STOCK (SEE SIDEBAR)

Continued...

DIRECTIONS

1. Preheat the oven to 250°F. Place the olive oil in a Dutch
    oven and warm it over medium heat. When the oil starts
    to shimmer, add the onion, garlic, parsnip, carrots, cumin,
    turmeric, and ginger and sauté for 2 minutes. Add the
    brisket and lamb and cook, stirring occasionally, until
    both are browned all over, about 8 minutes.

2. Add the stock and bring the mixture to a simmer. Stir in
    the chickpeas, potato, zucchini, tomatoes, lentils, bay leaf,
    and cilantro. Cover the pot, place it in the oven, and cook
    until the meat is very tender, about 1 hour.

3. Remove the stew from the oven and skim the fat from
    the surface. Season with salt and pepper and ladle the
    stew into warmed bowls. Garnish with the chilies and
    serve with the lemon wedges and rice.

BEEF STOCK

Place 3 lbs. rinsed beef bones in a large stockpot, cover them with water, and bring to a boil. Add 1 chopped onion, 2 chopped carrots, 3 chopped celery stalks, 3 unpeeled, smashed garlic cloves, 3 sprigs of fresh thyme, 1 teaspoon black peppercorns, 1 bay leaf, season the stock with salt, and reduce the heat so that the stock simmers. Cook for 2 hours, skimming to remove any impurities that float to the surface. Strain the stock through a fine sieve, let the stock cool slightly, and place it in the refrigerator, uncovered, to chill. Remove the fat layer and cover. The stock will keep in the refrigerator for 3 to 5 days, and in the freezer for up to 3 months.

½ CUP CHICKPEAS, SOAKED OVERNIGHT AND DRAINED

1 SMALL POTATO, PEELED AND CHOPPED

1 SMALL ZUCCHINI, SLICED

½ LB. TOMATOES, CHOPPED

2 TABLESPOONS BROWN LENTILS

1 BAY LEAF

½ BUNCH OF FRESH CILANTRO, CHOPPED

SALT AND PEPPER, TO TASTE

RED CHILI PEPPERS, STEMMED, SEEDS AND RIBS REMOVED, AND CHOPPED, FOR GARNISH

LEMON WEDGES, FOR SERVING

LONG-GRAIN RICE, COOKED, FOR SERVING

Gazpacho

INGREDIENTS

4 TOMATOES, CHOPPED, PLUS MORE FOR GARNISH

½ RED ONION, CHOPPED

½ CUCUMBER, CHOPPED, PLUS MORE FOR GARNISH

1 RED BELL PEPPER, STEMMED, SEEDS AND RIBS REMOVED, AND CHOPPED, PLUS MORE FOR GARNISH

1 CELERY STALK, CHOPPED

1 CUP CHOPPED DAY-OLD CRUSTY BREAD

2 TABLESPOONS FINELY CHOPPED FRESH PARSLEY

2 TABLESPOONS FINELY CHOPPED FRESH CHIVES

1 GARLIC CLOVE, MINCED

¼ CUP RED WINE VINEGAR

2 TABLESPOONS OLIVE OIL

1 TEASPOON FRESH LEMON JUICE

1 TEASPOON SUGAR

2 TEASPOONS TABASCO

1 TEASPOON WORCESTERSHIRE SAUCE

2 CUPS TOMATO JUICE

SALT AND PEPPER, TO TASTE

DIRECTIONS

1. Combine all of the ingredients in a large mixing bowl, cover, and place it in the refrigerator to chill overnight.

2. Transfer the soup to a food processor and blitz until it reaches the desired consistency. Chill in the refrigerator for 1 hour. Taste, adjust the seasoning if necessary, ladle into chilled bowls, and garnish with additional chopped vegetables.

Buttermilk Stew with Dumplings

YIELD: **6 SERVINGS**

ACTIVE TIME: **30 MINUTES**

TOTAL TIME: **45 MINUTES**

INGREDIENTS

FOR THE STEW

8 CUPS BUTTERMILK

½ CUP CHICKPEA FLOUR

1 TABLESPOON TURMERIC

1 TEASPOON KOSHER SALT

1 TABLESPOON OLIVE OIL

1 TEASPOON CORIANDER SEEDS

1 TABLESPOON BLACK
MUSTARD SEEDS

2 LARGE YELLOW ONIONS, HALVED
AND SLICED THIN

6 GARLIC CLOVES, MINCED

2-INCH PIECE OF FRESH GINGER,
PEELED AND MINCED

1 TEASPOON AMCHOOR POWDER

2 SERRANO PEPPERS, STEMMED,
SEEDS AND RIBS REMOVED,
AND MINCED

Continued...

DIRECTIONS

1. To begin preparations for the stew, place half of the buttermilk, the chickpea flour, turmeric, and salt in a food processor and blitz until smooth. Set the mixture aside.

2. Place the oil in a Dutch oven and warm it over high heat. When the oil starts to shimmer, add the coriander and mustard seeds and cook, stirring constantly, until they start to pop, about 2 minutes.

3. Reduce the heat to medium and add the onions, garlic, ginger, amchoor powder, and chili peppers. Sauté until the onions start to brown, about 10 minutes, and then pour in the buttermilk mixture. Add the remaining buttermilk, reduce the heat so that the stew gently simmers, and prepare the dumplings.

4. To prepare the dumplings, place the spinach, serrano peppers (if using), salt, red pepper flakes, and chaat masala in a mixing bowl and stir to combine. Add the chickpea flour and stir to incorporate. The dough should be quite stiff.

5. Roll tablespoons of the dough into balls and add them to the stew. When all of the dumplings have been added, cover the Dutch oven and simmer over low heat until the dumplings are cooked through, about 10 minutes. Ladle into warmed bowls and serve.

NOTE: Amchoor powder is made from the dried flesh of an unripe mango. Its sour flavor is crucial to North Indian cuisine, and you can find it at better grocery stores or online.

FOR THE DUMPLINGS

2 CUPS SPINACH, BLANCHED
AND CHOPPED

2 GREEN SERRANO PEPPERS,
STEMMED, SEEDS AND RIBS
REMOVED, AND MINCED
(OPTIONAL)

2 TEASPOONS KOSHER SALT

1 TEASPOON RED PEPPER FLAKES

1½ TEASPOONS CHAAT MASALA

1 CUP CHICKPEA FLOUR

Mediterranean Broccoli Soup

INGREDIENTS

1 TABLESPOON OLIVE OIL

1 TABLESPOON UNSALTED BUTTER

1 ONION, CHOPPED

1 GARLIC CLOVE, MINCED

1½ CUPS CHOPPED PORTOBELLO MUSHROOMS

1 BIRD'S EYE CHILI PEPPER, STEMMED, SEEDS AND RIBS REMOVED, AND CHOPPED

2 WHITE ANCHOVY FILLETS, MINCED

1 CUP CHOPPED TOMATOES

¼ CUP WHITE WINE

4 CUPS VEGETABLE STOCK (SEE PAGE 140)

2 CUPS BROCCOLI FLORETS

SALT AND PEPPER, TO TASTE

PARMESAN CHEESE, GRATED, FOR GARNISH

DIRECTIONS

1. Place the olive oil and butter in a saucepan and warm over medium heat. When the butter has melted, add the onion, garlic, mushrooms, chili, and anchovies and sauté until the onion starts to soften, about 5 minutes.

2. Stir in the tomatoes and the white wine and simmer, stirring occasionally, for 10 minutes.

3. Add the stock, raise the heat to medium-high, and bring the soup to a boil. Reduce the heat so that the soup simmers. Add the broccoli florets and cook for 10 minutes.

4. Season with salt and pepper, ladle the soup into warmed bowls, and garnish with Parmesan cheese.

YIELD: **6 SERVINGS**

ACTIVE TIME: **25 MINUTES**

TOTAL TIME: **1 HOUR**

Asparagus & Pea Soup

INGREDIENTS

¾ LB. ASPARAGUS

2 TABLESPOONS UNSALTED BUTTER

1 LEEK, TRIMMED, RINSED WELL, AND CHOPPED

1¼ CUPS PEAS, ¼ CUP RESERVED FOR GARNISH

1 TABLESPOON FINELY CHOPPED FRESH PARSLEY

5 CUPS VEGETABLE STOCK (SEE PAGE 140)

½ CUP HEAVY CREAM

ZEST OF 2 LEMONS, HALF RESERVED FOR GARNISH

SALT AND PEPPER, TO TASTE

FRESH MINT LEAVES, FOR GARNISH

PARMESAN CHEESE, SHAVED, FOR GARNISH

DIRECTIONS

1. Remove the woody ends of the asparagus and discard them. Separate the spears, remove the tips, set them aside, and chop what remains into 1-inch-long pieces.

2. Place the butter in a saucepan and melt it over medium heat. Add the leek and sauté until it starts to soften, about 5 minutes.

3. Add the chopped asparagus, the cup of peas, and the parsley. Cook for 3 minutes, stir in the stock, and bring to a boil. Reduce the heat so that the soup simmers and cook until the vegetables are tender, 6 to 8 minutes.

4. Transfer the soup to a blender, puree until smooth, and strain through a fine sieve.

5. Place the soup in a clean saucepan. Add the cream and lemon zest, season with salt and pepper, and bring to a simmer.

6. Bring a small pan of water to a boil and prepare an ice water bath. Place salt and the asparagus tips in the pan and cook until tender, 3 to 4 minutes. Remove the tips, submerge them in the ice water bath, pat dry with paper towels, and set aside.

7. Ladle the soup into warmed bowls and garnish with the asparagus tips, reserved peas, mint leaves, reserved lemon zest, and Parmesan.

Butternut Chicken Soup

INGREDIENTS

1 BUTTERNUT SQUASH, HALVED AND SEEDED

3 TABLESPOONS OLIVE OIL

2 CHICKEN BREASTS, CHOPPED

1 ONION, CHOPPED

2 GARLIC CLOVES, MINCED

4 CUPS CHICKEN STOCK (SEE PAGE 160)

1 (14 OZ.) CAN OF STEWED TOMATOES, DRAINED AND CHOPPED

1 TABLESPOON FINELY CHOPPED FRESH OREGANO

⅔ CUP QUINOA, RINSED

SALT AND PEPPER, TO TASTE

DIRECTIONS

1. Preheat the oven to 375°F. Place the butternut squash, cut side up, on a baking sheet, drizzle 2 tablespoons of the oil over it, and place it in the oven. Roast for 40 minutes, until the flesh is very tender. Remove from the oven and let cool.

2. Place the remaining oil in a Dutch oven and warm it over medium heat. When the oil starts to shimmer, add the chicken and cook, turning frequently, until it is browned all over, about 6 minutes. Remove the chicken with a slotted spoon and set it aside.

3. Add the onion to the pot and sauté until it starts to soften, about 5 minutes. Add the garlic, cook for 1 minute, and then add 3 cups of the stock, the stewed tomatoes, and the oregano. Bring to a boil and then reduce the heat so that the soup simmers.

4. Scoop the flesh of the butternut squash into a food processor or blender along with the remaining stock. Puree until smooth.

5. Add the butternut squash puree, chicken, and quinoa to the simmering broth. Cook until the quinoa is tender, about 15 minutes. Season with salt and pepper and ladle into warmed bowls.

Vegetable Soup with Couscous

YIELD: **4 SERVINGS**

ACTIVE TIME: **15 MINUTES**

TOTAL TIME: **45 MINUTES**

INGREDIENTS

2 TABLESPOONS OLIVE OIL

1 ONION, CHOPPED

1 LARGE CARROT, PEELED AND CHOPPED

1 (14 OZ.) CAN OF DICED TOMATOES, DRAINED

5 GARLIC CLOVES, MINCED

6 CUPS VEGETABLE STOCK (SEE PAGE 140)

1¼ CUPS ISRAELI COUSCOUS

¼ TEASPOON CUMIN

¼ CUP FINELY CHOPPED FRESH CILANTRO

SALT AND PEPPER, TO TASTE

⅛ TEASPOON CAYENNE PEPPER

DIRECTIONS

1. Place the olive oil in a large saucepan and warm over medium heat. When the oil starts to shimmer, add the onion and carrot and sauté until they start to soften, about 5 minutes.

2. Stir in the remaining ingredients and bring the soup to a boil. Reduce the heat so that it simmers and cook until the couscous is tender, about 10 minutes. Ladle the soup into warmed bowls.

CHAPTER 4

ENTREES

---

*Thanks to the wide-ranging vision supplied by New American
cuisine and the proliferation of fresh produce available locally, the age-
old argument that vegetable-based dishes are not as flavorful, filling, and
exciting as those that center around meat is ready to be put to rest.*

*No matter the season, no matter how proud a
carnivore someone claims to be, these dishes are ready to provide
vegetables their long overdue turn in the spotlight.*

Vegetarian Shepherd's Pie

YIELD: **6 SERVINGS**

ACTIVE TIME: **45 MINUTES**

TOTAL TIME: **1 HOUR AND 30 MINUTES**

INGREDIENTS

6 RUSSET POTATOES, PEELED AND CHOPPED

½ TEASPOON KOSHER SALT, PLUS MORE TO TASTE

11 TABLESPOONS UNSALTED BUTTER, DIVIDED INTO INDIVIDUAL TABLESPOONS

½ CUP MILK

¼ CUP PLAIN YOGURT

BLACK PEPPER, TO TASTE

1 SMALL ONION, MINCED

3 CUPS CHOPPED MUSHROOMS

1 BUNCH OF SWISS CHARD, CHOPPED

1 TABLESPOON WORCESTERSHIRE SAUCE

OLIVE OIL, AS NEEDED

DIRECTIONS

1. Preheat the oven to 350°F. Place the potatoes in a large saucepan and cover them with cold water. Bring the water to a boil, add the salt, and reduce the heat so that the potatoes simmer. Cook until fork-tender, about 20 minutes.

2. Drain the potatoes and place them in a large bowl. Add 6 tablespoons of the butter, the milk, and the yogurt and mash the potatoes until they are smooth and creamy. Season with salt and pepper and set aside.

3. In a large cast-iron skillet, melt 3 tablespoons of the butter over medium heat. Add the onion and sauté until translucent, about 3 minutes. Add the mushrooms, the chopped stems of the chard (not the leaves), and the Worcestershire sauce. Sauté for 3 minutes, reduce the heat to low, and cook until the mushrooms and chard stems are soft. If the pan seems dry, add a tablespoon of olive oil.

4. Raise the heat to medium and stir in the chard leaves. Cook, stirring constantly, until the leaves wilt, about 3 minutes. Remove the skillet from heat and season with salt and pepper.

5. Spread the mashed potatoes over the mixture, distributing the potatoes evenly and smoothing the top with a rubber spatula. Cut the remaining tablespoons of butter into slivers and dot the potatoes with them.

6. Cover the skillet with aluminum foil and bake for 25 minutes. Remove the foil and bake for another 10 minutes, until the topping is just browned and the filling is bubbly. Remove and briefly let cool before serving.

Slow-Cooker Quinoa & Veggies

YIELD: **6 SERVINGS**

ACTIVE TIME: **10 MINUTES**

TOTAL TIME: **5 HOURS**

INGREDIENTS

1½ CUPS QUINOA, RINSED

2½ CUPS VEGETABLE STOCK
(SEE PAGE 140)

1 YELLOW ONION, CHOPPED

½ RED BELL PEPPER, STEMMED,
SEEDS AND RIBS REMOVED,
AND CHOPPED

¾ LB. PORTOBELLO MUSHROOMS,
CHOPPED

2 GARLIC CLOVES, MINCED

1 TABLESPOON KOSHER SALT,
PLUS MORE TO TASTE

1 TABLESPOON BLACK PEPPER,
PLUS MORE TO TASTE

3 CUPS BABY SPINACH

1½ CUPS FRESH BASIL LEAVES,
CHOPPED

¼ CUP FINELY CHOPPED
FRESH DILL

2 TABLESPOONS FINELY CHOPPED
FRESH THYME

DIRECTIONS

1. Place all of the ingredients, except for the spinach and fresh herbs, in a slow cooker and cook on high until the quinoa is tender and slightly fluffy, about 4 hours.

2. Add the spinach and turn off the heat. Keep the slow cooker covered and let the mixture sit for 1 hour.

3. Fluff the quinoa with a fork, add the basil, dill, and thyme, and fold to incorporate. Season with salt and pepper and serve.

GUACAMOLE

Place the flesh of 3 avocados in a mixing bowl and mash. Stir in the juice of 2 limes, 2 seeded and chopped tomatoes, 1 chopped red onion, 2 minced garlic cloves, season with salt and pepper, and work the mixture until it is the desired texture. Garnish with finely chopped fresh cilantro and serve.

Veggie Burgers

INGREDIENTS

1 (14 OZ.) CAN OF BLACK BEANS, DRAINED AND RINSED

⅓ CUP MINCED SCALLIONS

¼ CUP CHOPPED ROASTED RED PEPPERS

¼ CUP CORN KERNELS

½ CUP PANKO

1 EGG, LIGHTLY BEATEN

2 TABLESPOONS FINELY CHOPPED FRESH CILANTRO

½ TEASPOON CUMIN

½ TEASPOON CAYENNE PEPPER

½ TEASPOON BLACK PEPPER

1 TEASPOON FRESH LIME JUICE

1 TABLESPOON OLIVE OIL

HAMBURGER BUNS, FOR SERVING

GUACAMOLE (SEE SIDEBAR), FOR SERVING

DIRECTIONS

1. Place half of the beans, the scallions, and roasted red peppers in a food processor and pulse until the mixture is a thick paste. Transfer it to a large bowl.

2. Add the corn, panko, egg, cilantro, cumin, cayenne, black pepper, and lime juice to the bowl and stir to combine. Add the remaining beans and stir until the mixture holds together.

3. Place the olive oil in a 12-inch cast-iron skillet and warm it over medium-high heat. Form the mixture into four patties. When the oil starts to shimmer, add the patties, cover the skillet, and cook until browned and cooked through, about 5 minutes per side. Serve on the hamburger buns with the Guacamole.

TIP: Should you be looking to avoid carbs or trying to use up some greens you have on hand, these veggie burgers are also wonderful served over arugula or mesclun greens.

YIELD: **6 SERVINGS**

ACTIVE TIME: **20 MINUTES**

TOTAL TIME: **1 HOUR**

Black Bean Burritos

INGREDIENTS

1 CUP BROWN RICE

¼ CUP CHOPPED FRESH CILANTRO

1 LARGE YELLOW SQUASH, SLICED THIN LENGTHWISE

1 LARGE ZUCCHINI, SLICED THIN LENGTHWISE

2 EARS OF CORN, SHUCKED

1 TABLESPOON OLIVE OIL

1 (14 OZ.) CAN OF BLACK BEANS, DRAINED AND RINSED

1 SMALL RED ONION, CHOPPED

2 TOMATOES, DICED

1 CUP SHREDDED RED CABBAGE

1 CUP GRATED PEPPER JACK CHEESE

6 LARGE FLOUR TORTILLAS

PINCH OF KOSHER SALT

SALSA VERDE (SEE SIDEBAR), FOR SERVING

DIRECTIONS

1. Begin by cooking the rice according to the instructions on the package. Once it has cooked completely, transfer it to a bowl, stir in the cilantro, and set aside.

2. Preheat your grill to 450°F. Brush the squash, zucchini, and corn with olive oil. Place on the grill and cook until they are charred and tender, about 10 minutes. Turn the vegetables while cooking and make sure they do not become too soft. Remove from heat and dice the zucchini and squash. Remove the corn kernels from the cobs and discard the cobs. Place the grilled vegetables in a bowl. Leave the grill on.

3. While the vegetables are grilling, warm the black beans in a saucepan.

4. Layer the rice-and-cilantro mixture, beans, grilled veggies, onion, tomatoes, cabbage, and cheese on the tortillas. Wrap tightly and place on the grill for about 1 minute per side. Remove from heat and serve with the Salsa Verde.

SALSA VERDE

Place 6 tomatillos and 8 serrano peppers in a large saucepan and cover them with water. Bring to a boil and cook until the tomatillos start to lose their bright green color, about 10 minutes. Drain and transfer the tomatillos and peppers to a blender. Add ½ chopped onion, 2 minced garlic cloves, salt to taste, and ¼ cup olive oil and puree until smooth. Top with finely chopped fresh cilantro and serve. The salsa will keep in the refrigerator for up to 2 days.

Celeriac Remoulade

INGREDIENTS

SALT AND WHITE PEPPER,
TO TASTE

1 LARGE CELERIAC, TRIMMED,
PEELED, AND GRATED

⅓ CUP MAYONNAISE

DASH OF TABASCO

1 TEASPOON DIJON MUSTARD

2 TEASPOONS FRESH LEMON JUICE

1 TEASPOON CAPERS

BIBB LETTUCE, FOR SERVING

4 OZ. SMOKED TROUT, TORN INTO
LARGE PIECES

FRESH CHIVES OR PARSLEY,
CHOPPED, FOR GARNISH

LEMON WEDGES, FOR SERVING

DIRECTIONS

1. Bring a medium saucepan of water to a boil. Add salt and the celeriac and cook for 1 minute. Drain, rinse with cold water, and let the celeriac drain completely.

2. Place the mayonnaise, Tabasco, mustard, lemon juice, and capers in a bowl and stir to combine.

3. Add the celeriac to the mayonnaise mixture, fold to incorporate, and season with salt and pepper.

4. Place a few lettuce leaves on each serving plate, place a mound of the remoulade on top, and top with a few pieces of the smoked trout. Garnish with chives or parsley and serve with a lemon wedge on the side.

Fried Eggplant Balls with Pasta

YIELD: **4 SERVINGS**

ACTIVE TIME: **45 MINUTES**

TOTAL TIME: **1 HOUR AND 30 MINUTES**

INGREDIENTS

2 LARGE EGGPLANTS, PEELED, TRIMMED, AND CHOPPED

¼ CUP OLIVE OIL, PLUS 1 TEASPOON

8 GARLIC CLOVES, UNPEELED

SALT AND PEPPER, TO TASTE

2¼ CUPS PANKO

1 CUP GRATED PARMESAN CHEESE, PLUS MORE FOR SERVING

2 HANDFULS OF FRESH PARSLEY LEAVES, CHOPPED

2 LARGE EGGS, LIGHTLY BEATEN

VEGETABLE OIL, AS NEEDED

¾ LB. PREFERRED PASTA

MARINARA SAUCE (SEE SIDEBAR)

¾ CUP WHOLE-MILK RICOTTA CHEESE

3 TABLESPOONS FINELY CHOPPED FRESH OREGANO

DIRECTIONS

1. Preheat the oven to 400°F and line two baking sheets with parchment paper. Place the eggplants in a bowl with the ¼ cup of the olive oil, toss to coat, and then place the eggplants on the baking sheets. Place the sheets in the oven and roast the eggplants, turning them occasionally, until golden brown, about 20 minutes. Remove one sheet from the oven, add the garlic, return to the oven, and bake until the skins of the garlic have turned a very light brownish color and opened, about 15 minutes. When done, remove from the oven, season with salt and pepper to taste, and mix well. When cool enough to handle, remove the garlic cloves from their skins and roughly chop them and the eggplants.

2. Place the eggplant-and-garlic mixture, 1½ cups of the panko, the Parmesan, two-thirds of the parsley, and the eggs in a bowl, season with salt and pepper, and stir to combine. Form the eggplant mixture into golf ball–sized spheres. Place the remaining panko in a small bowl and roll each sphere in it until coated evenly. Place the coated spheres on a plate or parchment-lined baking sheet.

3. Add vegetable oil to a large skillet or Dutch oven until it is ½ inch deep and warm it over medium heat. When the oil begins to shimmer, add the eggplant balls in batches. Fry, turning the balls gently as needed, until browned all over, 3 to 5 minutes per batch. Use a slotted spoon to transfer the cooked balls to a paper towel–lined plate and tent with aluminum foil to keep them warm.

Continued...

4. Bring a large pot of water to a boil. Add salt and the pasta and cook 2 minutes short of the directed cooking time. Reserve ¼ cup of the pasta water and drain. Return the empty pot to the stove, add the remaining oil and the reserved pasta water, and warm over high heat. Add the drained pasta and toss to combine. Add a few ladles of the sauce and cook, tossing continuously, for 2 minutes.

5. Divide the pasta among four warmed bowls and top with a little more sauce. Add a few dollops of ricotta and six of the eggplant balls to each portion, sprinkle with the oregano and a dusting of Parmesan, and serve.

Garlic Chicken

INGREDIENTS

8 BONELESS, SKINLESS
CHICKEN THIGHS

SALT AND PEPPER, TO TASTE

OLIVE OIL, AS NEEDED

8 WHITE OR BABY BELLA
MUSHROOMS, QUARTERED

40 GARLIC CLOVES

⅓ CUP DRY VERMOUTH

¾ CUP CHICKEN STOCK
(SEE PAGE 160)

1 TABLESPOON UNSALTED BUTTER

1 TABLESPOON FINELY CHOPPED
FRESH TARRAGON

BUTTERED EGG NOODLES OR
WHITE RICE, FOR SERVING

DIRECTIONS

1. Preheat the oven to 350°F. Generously season the chicken with salt and pepper and place it in a Dutch oven so that it is in one layer; cook in batches if necessary. Although oil is not necessarily needed when cooking chicken thighs, if the pan looks dry add a drizzle of olive oil. Cook over medium-high heat until browned, about 3 minutes. Turn the chicken over, and cook until browned on that side, about 3 minutes. Transfer the browned chicken thighs to a plate.

2. Place the mushrooms in the pot and sauté over medium heat until they start to brown, about 8 minutes. Add the garlic and sauté for 1 minute.

3. Deglaze the pot with the vermouth and stock, scrape the browned bits off the bottom of the pot, and then return the chicken to the Dutch oven.

4. Cover the Dutch oven with a lid, place the pot in the oven, and braise the chicken until tender and cooked through, about 25 minutes.

5. Remove the pot from the oven and transfer the chicken and mushrooms to a plate. With a wooden spoon, mash about half of the garlic cloves and stir to incorporate them into the pan sauce. If the sauce is thinner than you'd like, place the pot over medium-high heat and cook until it has reduced. Return the chicken and mushrooms to the pot, reduce the heat, and cook until warmed through.

6. When ready to serve, stir in the butter and tarragon and season to taste. Place one or two thighs and some mushrooms on a plate and spoon the sauce over the top, being sure to include both whole and mashed garlic cloves. Serve over buttered noodles or rice.

Tagliatelle with Veggies

YIELD: **4 TO 6 SERVINGS**

ACTIVE TIME: **50 MINUTES**

TOTAL TIME: **1 HOUR AND 30 MINUTES**

INGREDIENTS

1½ CUPS ALL-PURPOSE FLOUR, PLUS MORE AS NEEDED

1½ TEASPOONS KOSHER SALT, PLUS MORE TO TASTE

¾ CUP EGG YOLKS

1 TABLESPOON OLIVE OIL

BUNCH OF ASPARAGUS, TRIMMED AND CHOPPED

½ LB. SNAP PEAS, TRIMMED AND CHOPPED

4 TABLESPOONS UNSALTED BUTTER

¼ CUP GRATED PARMESAN CHEESE

½ TEASPOON RED PEPPER FLAKES

DIRECTIONS

1. Place the flour and salt in a mixing bowl, stir to combine, and make a well in the center. Pour the egg yolks and olive oil into the well and, starting in the center and gradually working to the outside, incorporate the flour into the well. When all the flour has been incorporated, place the dough on a flour-dusted work surface and knead until it is a smooth ball. Cover it in plastic wrap and let rest for 30 minutes.

2. Divide the dough into quarters. Use a rolling pin to flatten each quarter to a thickness that can go through the widest setting on a pasta maker.

3. Lightly dust several baking sheets with flour. Run the rolled pieces of dough through the pasta maker, adjusting the setting to reduce the thickness with each pass. Roll until you can see your hand through the dough. Cut the sheets into 10-inch-long pieces, dust them with flour, stack them on top of each other, and gently roll them up. Cut the roll into ¼-inch-wide strips, unroll them, and place the strips on the flour-dusted baking sheets.

4. Bring water to a boil in a medium saucepan and also in a large saucepan. Add salt, the asparagus, and peas to the medium saucepan and cook for 1 minute. Drain and set aside.

5. Add salt and the pasta to the large saucepan and cook for 3 to 4 minutes, stirring constantly. Reserve ¼ cup of the pasta water and then drain the pasta.

Continued...

6. Place the butter in a large skillet and melt over medium heat. Add the pasta and vegetables and toss to combine. Add the reserved pasta water, Parmesan, and red pepper flakes and toss to evenly coat. Season to taste and serve.

NOTE: If you don't have a pasta maker, roll out the dough as thin as it can get on a flour-dusted work surface and then cut it into 10-inch-long and ¼-inch-wide strips.

Fall Risotto

YIELD: **6 SERVINGS**

ACTIVE TIME: **35 MINUTES**

TOTAL TIME: **1 HOUR AND 20 MINUTES**

INGREDIENTS

1 STICK OF UNSALTED BUTTER

2 YELLOW ONIONS, CHOPPED

1 SMALL BUTTERNUT SQUASH, PEELED, SEEDED, AND CHOPPED

1 TABLESPOON KOSHER SALT, PLUS 2 TEASPOONS

3 CUPS WHOLE MILK

5 CUPS VEGETABLE STOCK (SEE PAGE 140)

2 CUPS ARBORIO RICE

2 CUPS WHITE WINE

3 CUPS BABY KALE, STEMMED AND CHOPPED

¾ CUP TOASTED WALNUTS

½ CUP DRIED CRANBERRIES

FRESH LEMON JUICE, TO TASTE

DIRECTIONS

1. Place 2 tablespoons of the butter in a saucepan and melt it over medium heat. Add one of the onions and sauté until it is translucent, about 3 minutes. Add the squash, the tablespoon of salt, and the milk, reduce the heat to low, and cook until the squash is tender, about 20 minutes. Strain, discard the cooking liquid, and transfer the squash and onion to a blender. Puree until smooth and then set aside.

2. Place the stock in a saucepan, bring it to a boil, and remove the pan from heat.

3. Place the remaining butter in a large skillet with high sides and melt it over medium heat. Add the remaining onion and sauté until translucent, about 3 minutes. Add the rice and remaining salt and cook, stirring constantly, until you can smell a toasted, nutty aroma. Be careful not to brown the rice.

4. Deglaze the pan with the white wine and continue to stir until all the liquid has been absorbed. Add the stock in 1-cup increments and stir constantly until all of the stock has been absorbed by the rice.

5. Add the squash puree and kale, stir to incorporate, and season to taste. Stir in the walnuts, dried cranberries, and lemon juice, and serve immediately.

Spicy Roasted Squash with Baby Kale Salad

YIELD: **4 SERVINGS**

ACTIVE TIME: **25 MINUTES**

TOTAL TIME: **2 HOURS**

INGREDIENTS

FOR THE SQUASH & SALAD

2 ACORN SQUASH

JERK MARINADE (SEE SIDEBAR)

1 TABLESPOON OLIVE OIL

½ TEASPOON KOSHER SALT

¼ TEASPOON BLACK PEPPER

¼ TEASPOON PAPRIKA

6 CUPS BABY KALE

½ CUP DRIED CRANBERRIES

1 CUP CRUMBLED FETA CHEESE

FOR THE MAPLE VINAIGRETTE

½ CUP APPLE CIDER VINEGAR

½ CUP REAL MAPLE SYRUP

1 TEASPOON ORANGE ZEST

2 TEASPOONS DIJON MUSTARD

1 TABLESPOON KOSHER SALT

1 TEASPOON BLACK PEPPER

2 ICE CUBES

1½ CUPS OLIVE OIL

DIRECTIONS

1. Preheat the oven to 400°F. To begin preparations for the squash and salad, halve the squash lengthwise, remove the seeds, and reserve them. Trim the ends of the squash so that each half can sit evenly, cut side up, on a baking sheet.

2. Score the squash's flesh in a crosshatch pattern, cutting approximately ⅛ inch deep. Brush some of the marinade on the squash and then fill the cavities with ⅓ cup.

3. Place the baking sheet in the oven and bake until the squash is tender, about 45 minutes to 1 hour. As the squash is cooking, baste the flesh with some of the marinade in the cavity every 15 minutes. Remove from the oven and let cool. Lower the oven's temperature to 350°F.

4. Run the squash seeds under water and remove any pulp. Pat the seeds dry, place them in a mixing bowl, and add the olive oil, salt, pepper, and paprika. Toss to combine and then place the seeds on a baking sheet. Place in the oven and bake until they are light brown and crispy, about 7 minutes.

5. Place the toasted seeds, kale, and cranberries in a salad bowl and toss to combine.

6. To prepare the vinaigrette, place all of the ingredients, except for the olive oil, in a food processor. Turn on high and add the oil in a slow stream. Puree until the mixture has emulsified. Season to taste and add to the salad bowl. Toss to coat and top the salad with the crumbled feta. To serve, place a bed of salad on each plate and place one of the roasted halves of squash on top.

JERK MARINADE

Place ¼ cup real maple syrup and brown sugar, 1 tablespoon molasses, fresh lime juice, and finely chopped fresh thyme, ½ teaspoon cayenne pepper, nutmeg, and ground cloves, 1 teaspoon chili powder, paprika, cumin, cinnamon, and black pepper, 2 teaspoons kosher salt and minced fresh ginger, 2 tablespoons sliced scallions and diced shallot, and 2 minced garlic cloves in a food processor and blitz until smooth.

Dry-Fried Beans

YIELD: **4 SERVINGS**

ACTIVE TIME: **15 MINUTES**

TOTAL TIME: **25 MINUTES**

INGREDIENTS

1 TABLESPOON OLIVE OIL,
PLUS MORE AS NEEDED

1 LB. GREEN BEANS, TRIMMED

½ LB. GROUND PORK

2 TABLESPOONS CHINESE PICKLED
VEGETABLES, CHOPPED

2 GARLIC CLOVES, CHOPPED

2 TABLESPOONS SHERRY

2 TABLESPOONS SOY SAUCE

1 TABLESPOON FERMENTED BLACK
BEAN GARLIC SAUCE

1 TEASPOON SUGAR

2 CUPS COOKED WHITE RICE,
FOR SERVING

DIRECTIONS

1. Place the oil in a large skillet and warm it over high heat. When the oil starts to shimmer, add the beans and let them cook until they start to char, about 5 minutes. Turn the beans over and cook on the other side until they are lightly charred all over. Transfer the beans to a bowl and set aside.

2. Add the pork to the pan and cook it over medium-high heat, breaking it up with a fork as it browns, for about 6 minutes. Add the pickled vegetables and the garlic. Cook, stirring continuously, until the contents of the pan are fragrant. Add more oil if the pan starts to look dry.

3. Add the sherry and cook until it has nearly evaporated. Stir in the soy sauce, fermented black bean garlic sauce, and sugar, return the green beans to the pan, and cook until heated through. Serve over the white rice.

NOTE: Depending on where you live, Chinese pickled vegetables may prove tough to come by, in which case either kimchi or sauerkraut can be comfortably substituted.

Halibut with Braised Vegetables

YIELD: **4 SERVINGS**

ACTIVE TIME: **30 MINUTES**

TOTAL TIME: **1 HOUR**

INGREDIENTS

¼ CUP OLIVE OIL

1 YELLOW BELL PEPPER, STEMMED, SEEDS AND RIBS REMOVED, AND CHOPPED

1 RED BELL PEPPER, STEMMED, SEEDS AND RIBS REMOVED, AND CHOPPED

1 HABANERO PEPPER, PIERCED

2 SMALL WHITE SWEET POTATOES, PEELED AND CHOPPED

1 CUP CHOPPED RED CABBAGE

3 GRAFFITI EGGPLANTS, CHOPPED

2-INCH PIECE OF FRESH GINGER, PEELED AND MASHED

4 GARLIC CLOVES, MINCED

2 TABLESPOONS GREEN CURRY PASTE

3 BABY BOK CHOY, CHOPPED

Continued...

DIRECTIONS

1. Place the olive oil in a Dutch oven and warm it over medium-high heat. When the oil starts to shimmer, add the bell peppers, habanero pepper, sweet potatoes, and cabbage. Season with salt and pepper and sauté until the sweet potatoes begin to caramelize, about 6 minutes.

2. Add the eggplants, ginger, and garlic and sauté until the eggplants begin to collapse, about 10 minutes. Stir in the curry paste and cook until the mixture is fragrant, about 2 minutes.

3. Add the bok choy, stock, paprika, cilantro, and coconut milk and cook until the liquid has reduced by one-quarter, about 20 minutes.

4. Add the kale to the Dutch oven. Place the halibut fillets on top of the kale, reduce the heat to medium, cover, and cook until the fish is cooked through, about 10 minutes.

5. Remove the Dutch oven's cover, remove the habanero, and discard it. Ladle the vegetables and the sauce into the bowls and top each portion with a halibut fillet. Garnish with the scallions and serve.

4 CUPS FISH STOCK (SEE SIDEBAR)

2 TABLESPOONS SWEET PAPRIKA

2 TABLESPOONS FINELY CHOPPED
FRESH CILANTRO

3 (14 OZ.) CANS OF COCONUT MILK

2 BUNCHES OF TUSCAN KALE,
STEMMED AND TORN

1½ LBS. HALIBUT FILLETS

SALT AND PEPPER, TO TASTE

SCALLIONS, TRIMMED AND
CHOPPED, FOR GARNISH

FISH STOCK

Place ¼ cup olive oil in a stockpot and warm over low heat. Add 1 trimmed, rinsed, and chopped leek, 1 unpeeled, chopped onion, 2 chopped carrots, and 1 chopped celery stalk and cook until the liquid they release has evaporated. Add ¾ lb. of whitefish bodies, 4 sprigs of fresh parsley, 3 sprigs of fresh thyme, 2 bay leaves, 1 teaspoon of black peppercorns and salt, and 8 cups water, raise the heat to high, and bring to a boil. Reduce heat so that the stock simmers and cook for 3 hours, while skimming to remove any impurities that float to the surface. Strain the stock through a fine sieve, let it cool slightly, and place in the refrigerator, uncovered, to chill. When the stock is completely cool, remove the fat layer from the top and cover. The stock will keep in the refrigerator for 3 to 5 days, and in the freezer for up to 3 months.

YIELD: **4 SERVINGS**

ACTIVE TIME: **40 MINUTES**

TOTAL TIME: **2 HOURS**

Ratatouille

INGREDIENTS

⅓ CUP OLIVE OIL

6 GARLIC CLOVES, MINCED

1 EGGPLANT, CHOPPED

2 ZUCCHINI, SLICED INTO
HALF-MOONS

2 BELL PEPPERS, STEMMED,
SEEDS AND RIBS REMOVED,
AND CHOPPED

4 TOMATOES, SEEDED
AND CHOPPED

SALT AND PEPPER, TO TASTE

DIRECTIONS

1. Place a large cast-iron skillet over medium-high heat and add half of the olive oil. When the oil starts to shimmer, add the garlic and eggplant and sauté until the vegetables are just starting to sizzle, about 2 minutes.

2. Reduce the heat to medium and stir in the zucchini, peppers, and remaining oil. Cover the skillet and cook, stirring occasionally, until the eggplant, zucchini, and peppers are almost tender, about 15 minutes.

3. Add the tomatoes, stir to combine, and cook until the eggplant, zucchini, and peppers are completely tender and the tomatoes have collapsed, about 25 minutes. Remove the skillet from heat, season with salt and pepper, and allow to sit for at least 1 hour. Reheat before serving.

Green Bean & Tofu Casserole

YIELD: **4 SERVINGS**

ACTIVE TIME: **10 MINUTES**

TOTAL TIME: **2 DAYS**

INGREDIENTS

FOR THE MARINADE

3 TABLESPOONS SOY SAUCE

2 TABLESPOONS RICE VINEGAR

1 TABLESPOON SESAME OIL

1 TABLESPOON HONEY

PINCH OF CINNAMON

PINCH OF BLACK PEPPER

FOR THE CASSEROLE

1 LB. EXTRA-FIRM TOFU, DRAINED AND CHOPPED

1 LB. GREEN BEANS

4 OZ. SHIITAKE MUSHROOMS, SLICED

2 TABLESPOONS SESAME OIL

1 TABLESPOON SOY SAUCE

2 TABLESPOONS SESAME SEEDS, FOR GARNISH

DIRECTIONS

1. To prepare the marinade, place all of the ingredients in a small bowl and stir to combine.

2. To begin preparations for the casserole, place the marinade and the tofu in a resealable plastic bag, place it in the refrigerator, and let it marinate for 2 days, gently shaking the bag occasionally.

3. Preheat the oven to 375°F. Remove the cubes of tofu from the bag. Place the green beans, mushrooms, sesame oil, and soy sauce in the bag and shake until the vegetables are coated.

4. Line a 9 x 13-inch baking pan with parchment paper and place the tofu on it in an even layer. Place in the oven and roast for 35 minutes. Remove the pan, flip the cubes of tofu over, and push them to the edge of the pan. Add the green bean-and-mushroom mixture, return the pan to the oven, and roast for 15 minutes, or until the green beans are cooked to your preference. Remove the pan from the oven, garnish with the sesame seeds, and serve.

Sweet & Spicy Roasted Barley

YIELD: **4 SERVINGS**

ACTIVE TIME: **20 MINUTES**

TOTAL TIME: **1 HOUR AND 30 MINUTES**

INGREDIENTS

5 CARROTS, PEELED AND CUT INTO 3-INCH PIECES

OLIVE OIL, TO TASTE

SALT AND PEPPER, TO TASTE

6 DRIED PASILLA PEPPERS

2¼ CUPS BOILING WATER

1 CUP PEARL BARLEY

1 RED ONION, MINCED

2 TABLESPOONS ADOBO SEASONING

1 TABLESPOON SUGAR

1 TABLESPOON CHILI POWDER

¼ CUP FINELY CHOPPED FRESH OREGANO

DIRECTIONS

1. Preheat the oven to 375°F. Place the carrots in a 9 x 13-inch baking pan, drizzle olive oil over them, and season with salt and pepper. Place in the oven and roast until the carrots are just soft to the touch, about 45 minutes.

2. While the carrots are cooking, open the Pasilla peppers and discard the seeds and stems. Place the peppers in a bowl, add the boiling water, and cover the bowl with aluminum foil.

3. When the carrots are cooked, remove the pan from the oven and add the remaining ingredients and the liquid the peppers have been soaking in. Chop the reconstituted peppers, add them to the pan, and spread the mixture so that the liquid is covering the barley. Cover the pan tightly with aluminum foil, place it in the oven, and bake until the barley is tender, about 45 minutes. Fluff with a fork and serve immediately.

Noodles with Marinated Eggplant & Tofu

YIELD: **4 SERVINGS**

ACTIVE TIME: **45 MINUTES**

TOTAL TIME: **1 HOUR AND 45 MINUTES**

INGREDIENTS

FOR THE MARINADE

2 TABLESPOONS RICE VINEGAR

3 TABLESPOONS SOY SAUCE

1 TABLESPOON TOASTED SESAME OIL

½ TEASPOON SUGAR

2 GARLIC CLOVES, MINCED

FOR THE DRESSING

1 TABLESPOON RICE VINEGAR

1 TABLESPOON PEANUT OIL

1 TEASPOON SOY SAUCE

1 TABLESPOON TOASTED SESAME OIL

1-INCH PIECE OF FRESH GINGER, PEELED AND GRATED

FOR THE NOODLES

2 LBS. EGGPLANTS

½ LB. SOBA NOODLES

3 TABLESPOONS PEANUT OIL

SALT, TO TASTE

¾ LB. EXTRA-FIRM TOFU, DRAINED AND DICED

6 SCALLIONS, TRIMMED AND CHOPPED, FOR GARNISH

DIRECTIONS

1. To prepare the marinade, place all of the ingredients in a small bowl and stir to combine. To prepare the dressing, place all of the ingredients in a separate small bowl and stir to combine. Set the marinade and the dressing aside.

2. To begin preparations for the noodles, trim the eggplants, slice them in half, and cut them into ½-inch cubes. Place in a mixing bowl, add the marinade, and toss to combine. Let stand for 1 hour at room temperature.

3. Bring a large pot of water to a boil. Add the noodles and stir for the first minute to prevent any sticking. Cook until tender but still chewy, about 4 minutes. Drain, rinse under cold water, drain again, and place the noodles in a large bowl. Add the dressing, toss to coat, and set aside.

4. Warm a wok or a large skillet over medium heat for 2 to 3 minutes. Raise the heat to medium-high and add 2 tablespoons of the peanut oil. When it begins to shimmer, add the eggplant and a couple pinches of salt and stir-fry until the eggplant softens and starts to brown, 5 to 6 minutes. Using a slotted spoon, transfer the eggplant to a paper towel–lined plate. Add the remaining peanut oil and the tofu cubes to the pan and stir-fry until they turn golden brown all over, 4 to 5 minutes. Using a slotted spoon, transfer the tofu to a separate paper towel–lined plate.

5. Divide the soba noodles between four bowls. Arrange the eggplant and tofu on top and garnish with the scallions.

Vegetarian Lasagna

INGREDIENTS

1 CUP DRY RED WINE

2 TABLESPOONS UNSALTED BUTTER

3 SHALLOTS, MINCED

SALT AND PEPPER, TO TASTE

2 GARLIC CLOVES, PEELED
AND MINCED

1 LB. CREMINI MUSHROOMS,
STEMMED AND SLICED THIN

1 OZ. DRIED PORCINI
MUSHROOMS, RECONSTITUTED
AND CHOPPED, SOAKING
LIQUID RESERVED

2 TABLESPOONS FINELY CHOPPED
FRESH THYME, PLUS MORE
FOR GARNISH

BÉCHAMEL SAUCE (SEE SIDEBAR)

½ LB. DRIED LASAGNA NOODLES

1½ CUPS GRATED PARMESAN
CHEESE

DIRECTIONS

1. Place the wine in a small saucepan and bring it to a boil. Cook until it has reduced almost by half, about 5 minutes. Remove the pan from heat and set it aside.

2. Warm a large, deep skillet over medium heat for 2 to 3 minutes and then add the butter. When the butter has melted, add the shallots and a pinch of salt and stir. Once the shallots begin to sizzle, reduce the temperature to low, cover the pan, and cook, stirring occasionally, until they have softened, about 10 minutes. Stir in the garlic and cook for 30 seconds.

3. Raise the heat to medium-high, add the cremini and porcini mushrooms and the thyme, season with salt, and stir. Sauté until the mushrooms begin to release their liquid, about 5 minutes. Add the reduced wine, the porcini soaking liquid, and a pinch of salt and bring to a gentle simmer. Cook, stirring occasionally, until the mushrooms are tender and the liquid has reduced by half, 12 to 15 minutes. Remove the pan from heat, season to taste, and then stir in the Béchamel Sauce.

4. Preheat the oven to 350°F. Bring a large pot of water to a boil. Once it's boiling, add salt and the lasagna sheets and cook until just slightly tender, about 5 minutes. Transfer the cooked sheets to a large bowl of cold water, allow them to cool completely, drain, and place them on paper towels to dry.

Continued...

BÉCHAMEL SAUCE

Place 2 tablespoons unsalted butter in a saucepan and melt it over low heat. Add 2 tablespoons flour, whisk to combine, and cook for 1 minute. Gradually add 1 cup milk, whisking constantly to prevent lumps from forming. Continue whisking until the sauce has thickened, about 5 minutes. Add salt and pepper to taste and a pinch of freshly grated nutmeg, stir to incorporate, and serve.

5. Cover the bottom of a deep 9 x 13-inch baking pan with the mushroom mixture. Cover with a layer of noodles, making sure they are slightly overlapping. Cover with a layer of the mushroom mixture and sprinkle ½ cup of the Parmesan on top. Repeat this layering two more times, ending with a layer of the mushroom mixture topped with the remaining Parmesan. Cover the pan loosely with aluminum foil, place it in the oven, and bake for 35 minutes. Remove the foil and continue to bake until the edges of the lasagna sheets are lightly browned, about 12 minutes. For nice, clean slices, remove the lasagna from the oven and allow it to rest for at least 20 minutes before slicing.

YIELD: **4 SERVINGS**

ACTIVE TIME: **15 MINUTES**

TOTAL TIME: **30 MINUTES**

Saag Aloo

INGREDIENTS

1 TABLESPOON OLIVE OIL

½ LB. FINGERLING OR RED POTATOES, PEELED AND CHOPPED

1 ONION, CHOPPED

1 TEASPOON MUSTARD SEEDS

1 TEASPOON CUMIN

1 GARLIC CLOVE, CHOPPED

1-INCH PIECE OF FRESH GINGER, PEELED AND MINCED

1 LB. FROZEN CHOPPED SPINACH

1 TEASPOON RED PEPPER FLAKES

½ CUP WATER

SALT, TO TASTE

2 TABLESPOONS PLAIN YOGURT, OR TO TASTE

DIRECTIONS

1. Place the olive oil in a large skillet and warm it over medium heat. When the oil starts to shimmer, add the potatoes and cook until they start to brown, about 5 minutes.

2. Add the onion, mustard seeds, and cumin and sauté until the onion starts to soften, about 5 minutes. Add the garlic and ginger and cook, stirring constantly, until the mixture is fragrant, about 2 minutes.

3. Stir in the frozen spinach, the red pepper flakes, and water and cover the pan with a lid. Cook, stirring occasionally, until the spinach is heated through, about 10 minutes.

4. Remove the cover and cook until all of the liquid has evaporated. Season with salt, stir in the yogurt, and serve. Add more yogurt if you prefer a creamier dish.

Green Spätzle with Gorgonzola Cream

INGREDIENTS

FOR THE SPÄTZLE

2 LBS. SWISS CHARD

1½ TABLESPOONS KOSHER SALT, PLUS MORE TO TASTE

4 LARGE EGGS

1 TEASPOON FRESHLY GRATED NUTMEG

2 CUPS ALL-PURPOSE FLOUR, PLUS MORE AS NEEDED

¼ CUP WATER

MILK, AS NEEDED

OLIVE OIL, AS NEEDED

FOR THE GORGONZOLA CREAM

2 CUPS HEAVY CREAM

4 OZ. GORGONZOLA DOLCE CHEESE, CHOPPED

⅔ CUP GRATED PARMESAN CHEESE

1 TEASPOON FRESHLY GRATED NUTMEG

SALT AND WHITE PEPPER, TO TASTE

DIRECTIONS

1. To begin preparations for the spätzle, remove the stems from the chard and discard them. Bring a large pot of water to a boil. Add salt and the chard leaves and cook until wilted, about 3 minutes. Using a strainer, transfer the greens to a colander set in a large bowl. Reserve the water to cook the spätzle.

2. Rinse the chard under cold water, drain, and squeeze the leaves to remove as much liquid as possible from them. Place them on paper towels and pat dry.

3. Place the chard, eggs, 1½ tablespoons salt, and nutmeg in a food processor and pulse until the chard is shredded. Add the flour and water and blitz until the mixture is smooth, about 3 minutes, stopping to scrape down the work bowl as necessary. Transfer the batter to a mixing bowl. At this point, the dough should be more like pancake batter; if it seems too thick, add milk, 1 teaspoon at a time, until it has the right consistency. Cover with plastic wrap and let rest for 1 hour at room temperature.

4. To prepare the gorgonzola cream, place the cream and cheeses in a medium saucepan and cook, stirring occasionally, over medium heat until the cream is gently simmering and the sauce is smooth, about 5 minutes. Continue to simmer the sauce until it is thick enough to coat the back of a wooden spoon, 8 to 9 minutes. Stir in the nutmeg, season with salt and white pepper, and set aside.

Continued...

5. Bring the pot of water you used to cook the greens in back to a boil. Reduce heat so the water gently boils. Grease a spätzle maker with nonstick cooking spray and push handfuls of the dough through it into the boiling water. Stir the pot from time to time with a long wooden spoon to dislodge any spätzle stuck to the bottom. Cook until they float to the surface, about 1 minute. Quickly remove them with a strainer and transfer to a parchment-lined baking sheet. Drizzle olive oil over the spätzle so that they don't stick together and tent loosely with aluminum foil to keep them warm. Repeat until all of the spätzle have been cooked and serve with Gorgonzola Cream.

Maple-Roasted Vegetables with Caramelized Onions & Mashed Potatoes

YIELD: **4 SERVINGS**

ACTIVE TIME: **25 MINUTES**

TOTAL TIME: **1 HOUR**

INGREDIENTS

1 STICK OF UNSALTED BUTTER, PLUS MORE FOR SERVING

4 LARGE ONIONS, SLICED

1 RUTABAGA, TRIMMED, PEELED, AND DICED

1 BUNCH OF BEETS, TRIMMED, PEELED, AND DICED

2 LARGE CARROTS, PEELED AND DICED

2 TABLESPOONS OLIVE OIL

3 TABLESPOONS REAL MAPLE SYRUP

SALT AND PEPPER, TO TASTE

1½ LBS. POTATOES, PEELED AND DICED

¾ CUP HEAVY CREAM

DIRECTIONS

1. Preheat the oven to 375°F. Melt 3 tablespoons of the butter in a skillet over medium-high heat and add the onions. Raise heat to high and sauté the onions for 2 minutes. Reduce heat to low and cook, stirring occasionally, until the onions have caramelized, 30 to 40 minutes.

2. While the onions are cooking, place the rutabaga, beets, carrots, olive oil, maple syrup, salt, and pepper in a bowl and toss to combine. Spread the mixture in an even layer in a roasting pan and place the pan in the oven. Roast until the vegetables are browned, turning them occasionally, about 45 minutes.

3. While the vegetables are roasting, place the potatoes in a large saucepan and cover with water. Bring to a boil and cook until tender, about 15 minutes. Drain and immediately transfer to a large mixing bowl. Add 2½ tablespoons of the butter and half of the cream. Mash to combine the ingredients. Once the potatoes are slightly mashed, add the remaining butter and cream, season with salt and pepper, and mash until smooth and creamy.

4. To serve, place a dollop of the mashed potatoes on a plate and make a well in the center. Spoon some of the roasted vegetables into the well and top with a spoonful of caramelized onions and additional butter.

Spaghetti Squash Noodles

YIELD: **4 SERVINGS**

ACTIVE TIME: **30 MINUTES**

TOTAL TIME: **1 HOUR AND 15 MINUTES**

INGREDIENTS

2 SPAGHETTI SQUASH

SALT AND WHITE PEPPER, TO TASTE

1 LB. SWISS CHARD, STEMMED

½ CUP PECANS

3 TABLESPOONS OLIVE OIL, PLUS 2 TEASPOONS

1 TEASPOON CHILI POWDER

1 TEASPOON SUGAR

2 GARLIC CLOVES, MINCED

½ TEASPOON RED PEPPER FLAKES

1 TABLESPOON FINELY CHOPPED FRESH ROSEMARY

1 TEASPOON CHINESE BLACK VINEGAR

¾ CUP GRATED PARMESAN CHEESE

DIRECTIONS

1. Preheat the oven to 400°F. Line a large baking pan with aluminum foil and trim a sheet of parchment paper so that it fits in the bottom of the pan. Trim the ends of the squash, scrape out the seeds, and cut each one into four rounds. Place them in the pan, place the pan in the oven, and roast until the strands are tender but still firm, about 50 minutes. Remove from the oven and let the squash cool for 10 minutes.

2. Using a fork, pull the strands in the center of each round to create long strands of "spaghetti." Working in two batches, transfer half of the strands to a kitchen towel and gently wring it to remove as much liquid from the squash as possible. Transfer the squash to a large bowl and repeat this step with the other half of the squash. Set aside.

3. While the squash is roasting, bring a large pot of water to a boil. Add salt and the chard leaves and cook until wilted, about 2 minutes. Using a strainer, transfer to a colander and rinse under cold water until cool. Drain, squeeze the chard to remove as much liquid as possible, and mince. Set aside.

4. Place the pecans in a small resealable bag and gently crush them with a rolling pin. Warm a skillet for 3 minutes over low heat. Add the 2 teaspoons of olive oil, the chili powder, and sugar and stir. Once the mixture starts to sizzle, add the pecans and stir until coated. Cook until fragrant, about 2 minutes. Season with salt, transfer to a plate, and let cool.

Continued...

5. Warm a large skillet over low heat for 2 to 3 minutes. Add 1 tablespoon of the oil and warm for a minute, then add the garlic, red pepper flakes, rosemary, and a pinch of salt. Cook until the garlic just starts to brown, about 1 minute. Raise the heat to medium-high, add the chard and a pinch of salt, stir to combine, and cook for 3 minutes. Transfer the mixture to a warmed bowl and tent with aluminum foil to keep warm. Add the remaining olive oil and let it warm for a minute. Add the spaghetti squash strands and two pinches of salt and toss to coat. Sprinkle the vinegar over the top, season with white pepper, and toss again. Taste and adjust the seasoning as needed. Remove the pan from heat, add the Parmesan, and toss to combine. Divide between four warm bowls and top with the chard and pecans.

Sweet Potato Gnocchi

INGREDIENTS

2½ LBS. SWEET POTATOES

½ CUP RICOTTA CHEESE

1 EGG

2 EGG YOLKS

1 TABLESPOON KOSHER SALT, PLUS MORE TO TASTE

1 TEASPOON BLACK PEPPER

3 TABLESPOONS LIGHT BROWN SUGAR

2 TABLESPOONS REAL MAPLE SYRUP

2 CUPS ALL-PURPOSE FLOUR, PLUS MORE AS NEEDED

1 CUP SEMOLINA FLOUR

2 TABLESPOONS OLIVE OIL

1 STICK OF UNSALTED BUTTER

1 TABLESPOON FINELY CHOPPED FRESH SAGE

2 CUPS ARUGULA

½ CUP TOASTED WALNUTS, CHOPPED

DIRECTIONS

1. Preheat the oven to 350°F. Wash the sweet potatoes, place them on a parchment-lined baking sheet, and use a knife to pierce several holes in the tops of the potatoes. Place in the oven and bake until they are soft all the way through, 45 minutes to 1 hour. Remove from the oven, slice them open, and let cool completely.

2. Scrape the cooled sweet potato flesh into a mixing bowl and mash until smooth. Add the ricotta, egg, egg yolks, salt, pepper, brown sugar, and maple syrup and stir until thoroughly combined. Add the flours 1 cup at a time and work the mixture with your hands until incorporated. The dough should not feel sticky when touched. If it is too sticky, incorporate additional all-purpose flour 1 teaspoon at a time until it has the right texture. Place the olive oil in a mixing bowl and set aside.

3. Transfer the dough to a flour-dusted work surface and cut it into 10 even pieces. Roll each piece into a long rope and cut the ropes into ¾-inch-wide pieces. Use a fork to roll the gnocchi into the desired shape and place the shaped dumplings on a flour-dusted baking sheet.

4. Bring a large pot of water to boil. Add salt, and then add the gnocchi in small batches, stirring to keep them from sticking to the bottom. The gnocchi will eventually float to the surface. Cook for 1 more minute, remove, and transfer to the bowl containing the olive oil. Toss to coat and place on a parchment-lined baking sheet to cool.

5. Place the butter in a skillet and warm over medium heat until it begins to brown. Add the sage and cook until the bubbles start to dissipate. Place the arugula in a bowl and set it aside.

6. Working in batches, add the gnocchi to the skillet, toss to coat, and cook until they have a nice sear on one side. Transfer to the bowl of arugula and toss to combine. Plate and top with the toasted walnuts.

Coconut Kuri Curry

INGREDIENTS

3 TABLESPOONS OLIVE OIL

1½ LBS. RED KURI SQUASH, PEELED AND CUBED

1 ONION, CHOPPED

2 GARLIC CLOVES, CHOPPED

1-INCH PIECE OF FRESH GINGER, PEELED AND MINCED

1 TEASPOON CUMIN

1 TEASPOON CORIANDER

½ TEASPOON FENNEL SEEDS

PINCH OF CAYENNE PEPPER (OPTIONAL)

½ TEASPOON TURMERIC

½ CUP COCONUT MILK

½ CUP WATER

1 TABLESPOON TAMARIND PASTE

2 CUPS FRESH BABY SPINACH

SALT AND PEPPER, TO TASTE

WHITE RICE, FOR SERVING

DIRECTIONS

1. Place the oil in a large skillet and warm it over medium-high heat. When the oil starts to shimmer, add the squash and cook until it just starts to brown, about 5 minutes.

2. Add the onion, garlic, and ginger and cook until the onion starts to soften, about 5 minutes. Stir in the cumin, coriander, fennel seeds, cayenne (if using), turmeric, coconut milk, water, and tamarind paste and allow the mixture to return to a simmer. Reduce the heat to low and cook until the squash is tender, about 10 minutes.

3. In the last 5 minutes of cooking, stir in the spinach. Season with salt and pepper and serve with white rice.

Southwestern Polenta

INGREDIENTS

1 TABLESPOON OLIVE OIL, PLUS MORE AS NEEDED

1 ONION, CHOPPED

1 CUP CORN KERNELS

½ BELL PEPPER, STEMMED, SEEDS AND RIBS REMOVED, AND CHOPPED

1 SMALL JALAPEÑO PEPPER, STEMMED, SEEDS AND RIBS REMOVED, AND CHOPPED (OPTIONAL)

½ LB. TOMATILLOS, HUSKED, RINSED, AND CHOPPED

1 TEASPOON CUMIN

1½ TEASPOONS KOSHER SALT

1 GARLIC CLOVE, MINCED

1 CUP MILK

2 CUPS WATER, PLUS MORE AS NEEDED

1 CUP MEDIUM-GRAIN CORNMEAL

2 TABLESPOONS UNSALTED BUTTER

1 CUP GRATED CHEDDAR CHEESE, PLUS MORE FOR GARNISH

FRESH CILANTRO, FINELY CHOPPED, FOR GARNISH

DIRECTIONS

1. Place the oil in a large skillet and warm it over medium-high heat. When the oil starts to shimmer, add the onion and sauté until it starts to brown, about 5 minutes. Add the corn and continue to cook, adding more oil if the pan becomes too dry. When the corn has started to brown, add the bell pepper, jalapeno (if using), tomatillos, cumin, and 1 teaspoon of the salt. Cook until the tomatillos start to collapse, about 8 minutes. Add the garlic and cook until fragrant, about 2 minutes. Remove the pan from heat and set it aside.

2. Place the milk, water, and remaining salt in a medium saucepan and bring it to a boil. Add the cornmeal gradually, while stirring constantly to prevent lumps from forming. Reduce the heat so that the mixture simmers, stirring continuously. Continue until all of the liquid is absorbed and the cornmeal is tender, about 20 minutes. If the polenta absorbs all of the water before it is tender, add up to 1 cup water.

3. Stir the butter and cheese into the polenta. To serve, ladle the polenta onto a plate and top with a large spoonful of the corn-and-tomatillo mixture. Garnish with the cilantro and additional cheddar cheese.

YIELD: **4 SERVINGS**

ACTIVE TIME: **1 HOUR AND 15 MINUTES**

TOTAL TIME: **2 HOURS**

Moussaka

INGREDIENTS

FOR THE FILLING

4 CUPS COLD WATER

¼ CUP KOSHER SALT, PLUS MORE
TO TASTE

1 LARGE EGGPLANT, TRIMMED AND
SLICED

5 TABLESPOONS OLIVE OIL

1 LB. GROUND LAMB

1 ONION, DICED

3 GARLIC CLOVES, MINCED

½ CUP DRY RED WINE

1 CUP TOMATO SAUCE

2 TABLESPOONS FINELY CHOPPED
FRESH PARSLEY

1 TEASPOON DRIED OREGANO

½ TEASPOON CINNAMON

BLACK PEPPER, TO TASTE

FOR THE CRUST

5 EGGS

6 TABLESPOONS UNSALTED BUTTER

⅓ CUP ALL-PURPOSE FLOUR

2½ CUPS MILK

⅔ CUP GRATED PARMESAN CHEESE

⅓ CUP CHOPPED FRESH DILL OR
PARSLEY, CHOPPED

DIRECTIONS

1. Preheat the oven to 350°F. To begin preparations for the filling, place the cold water in a bowl, add the salt, and stir. When the salt has dissolved, add the eggplant and let it soak for about 20 minutes. Drain the eggplant and rinse with cold water. Squeeze the eggplant to remove as much water as you can, place it on a pile of paper towels, and pat it dry. Set aside.

2. While the eggplant is soaking, place a tablespoon of the olive oil in a large cast-iron skillet and warm it over medium-high heat. When the oil starts to shimmer, add the ground lamb and cook, using a fork to break it up, until it is browned, about 8 minutes. Transfer the cooked lamb to a bowl and set it aside.

3. Add 2 tablespoons of the olive oil and the eggplant to the skillet and cook, stirring frequently, until it starts to brown, about 5 minutes. Transfer the cooked eggplant to the bowl containing the lamb and add the rest of the oil, the onion, and the garlic to the skillet. Sauté until the onion is translucent, about 3 minutes, return the lamb and eggplant to the skillet, and stir in the wine, tomato sauce, parsley, oregano, and cinnamon. Reduce the heat to low and simmer for about 15 minutes, stirring occasionally. Season with salt and pepper and remove the pan from heat.

4. To begin preparations for the crust, place the eggs in a large bowl and beat them lightly. Place a saucepan over medium heat, add the butter, and melt it. Reduce the heat to medium-low and add the flour. Stir constantly until the mixture is smooth.

Continued...

5. While stirring constantly, gradually add the milk and bring the mixture to a boil. When the mixture reaches a boil, remove the pan from heat. Stir approximately half of the mixture in the saucepan into the beaten eggs. Stir the tempered eggs into the saucepan and then add the cheese and dill or parsley. Stir to combine and pour the mixture over the lamb- and-eggplant mixture in the skillet, using a rubber spatula to smooth the top.

6. Place the skillet in the oven and bake until the crust is set and golden brown, about 35 minutes. Remove from the oven and let the moussaka rest for 5 minutes before serving.

Tarhana

INGREDIENTS

6 PLUM TOMATOES

3 TABLESPOONS OLIVE OIL

1 ONION, MINCED

¼ TEASPOON KOSHER SALT, PLUS MORE TO TASTE

1 GARLIC CLOVE, MINCED

1½ LBS. FRESH GREEN BEANS, TRIMMED

1½ CUPS VEGETABLE STOCK (SEE PAGE 140), PLUS MORE AS NEEDED

⅔ CUP TARHANA

¼ CUP FRESH BASIL LEAVES, SHREDDED

BLACK PEPPER, TO TASTE

DIRECTIONS

1. Bring water to a boil in a medium saucepan. Add the tomatoes and boil for 1 minute. Use tongs to transfer them to a cutting board and let them cool. When cool enough to handle, peel the tomatoes and discard the skins. Cut the tomatoes into quarters, remove the seeds and discard them, and chop the flesh.

2. Warm a large, deep skillet over medium-low heat for 2 to 3 minutes. Add the olive oil and raise the heat to medium. When it begins to shimmer, add the onion and a couple pinches of salt and sauté until the onion begins to sizzle. Reduce the heat to low, cover, and cook until the onion is very soft, about 15 minutes. Add the garlic and sauté for 1 minute. Stir in the tomatoes and a couple pinches of salt and raise the heat to medium-high. Once the sauce begins to bubble, reduce the heat to low, cover the pan, and cook, stirring occasionally, until the tomatoes start to collapse, about 10 minutes.

3. Add the green beans, stock, the ¼ teaspoon of salt, and the tarhana. Raise the heat to medium-high and bring the mixture to a gentle simmer. Reduce heat to medium-low and cook, stirring occasionally, until the green beans and tarhana are tender, 15 to 20 minutes. Add more stock as necessary.

4. Season to taste, remove the pan from heat, and stir in the basil and black pepper. You can serve this preparation hot or at room temperature.

Stuffed Eggplants

INGREDIENTS

2 LARGE EGGPLANTS, HALVED

2 TABLESPOONS OLIVE OIL, PLUS MORE AS NEEDED

½ CUP QUINOA, RINSED

1 CUP WATER

2 ONIONS, CHOPPED

3 GARLIC CLOVES, MINCED

2 BELL PEPPERS, STEMMED, SEEDS AND RIBS REMOVED, AND CHOPPED

1 LB. GROUND LAMB

SALT AND PEPPER, TO TASTE

½ TEASPOON GARAM MASALA

2 TEASPOONS CUMIN

FRESH PARSLEY, FINELY CHOPPED, FOR GARNISH

DIRECTIONS

1. Preheat the oven to 400°F. Place the eggplants on a baking sheet, drizzle olive oil over the top, and place them in the oven. Roast until the flesh is tender, about 30 minutes. Remove from the oven and let the eggplants cool slightly. When cool enough to handle, scoop out the flesh, mince it, and place it in a mixing bowl. Set the hollowed-out eggplants aside and leave the oven on.

2. Place the quinoa and water in a saucepan and bring to a boil over medium heat. Let the quinoa boil until it has absorbed all of the water. Remove the pan from heat, cover it, and let it steam for 5 minutes. Fluff with a fork and let cool slightly.

3. Place the olive oil in a large skillet and warm it over medium-high heat. When the oil starts to shimmer, add the onions, garlic, and bell pepper and sauté until the onions and pepper start to soften, about 5 minutes. Add the ground lamb, season it with salt and pepper, stir in the garam masala and cumin, and cook, breaking the lamb up with a fork, until it is browned, about 6 minutes. Transfer the mixture to the bowl containing the minced eggplant. Add the quinoa to the bowl and stir until the mixture is combined.

4. Fill the cavities of the hollowed-out eggplants with the lamb-and-quinoa mixture. Place them on a baking sheet, place them in the oven, and roast until they are starting to collapse, about 15 minutes. Remove from the oven and let them cool slightly before garnishing with the parsley and serving.

Briam

INGREDIENTS

3 YUKON GOLD POTATOES,
PEELED AND SLICED THIN

3 ZUCCHINI, SLICED THIN

SALT AND PEPPER, TO TASTE

1 TABLESPOON FINELY CHOPPED
FRESH OREGANO

2 TEASPOONS FINELY CHOPPED
FRESH ROSEMARY

½ CUP FRESH PARSLEY, CHOPPED

4 GARLIC CLOVES, MINCED

3 TABLESPOONS OLIVE OIL

4 TOMATOES, SEEDED
AND CHOPPED

1 LARGE RED ONION, HALVED
AND SLICED THIN

DIRECTIONS

1. Preheat the oven to 400°F. Place the potatoes and zucchini in a bowl, season with salt and pepper, and then add the oregano, rosemary, parsley, garlic, and olive oil. Stir until the vegetables are evenly coated and set aside.

2. Cover the bottom of a 10-inch cast-iron skillet with half of the tomatoes. Arrange the potatoes, zucchini, and onion in rows, working in from the edge of the pan to the center and alternating the vegetables as you go. Top with the remaining tomatoes and cover with foil.

3. Place the skillet in the oven and roast for 45 minutes. Remove from the oven, remove the foil, and roast for another 40 minutes, until the vegetables are charred and tender. Remove from the oven and let cool briefly before serving.

Roasted Chicken, Roots & Brassicas

YIELD: **4 SERVINGS**

ACTIVE TIME: **30 MINUTES**

TOTAL TIME: **24 HOURS**

INGREDIENTS

1½ GALLONS CHICKEN BRINE (SEE SIDEBAR)

5-LB. WHOLE CHICKEN

SALT AND PEPPER, TO TASTE

1 TABLESPOON FINELY CHOPPED FRESH THYME

1 SWEET POTATO, PEELED AND CHOPPED

1 CUP CHOPPED CELERY ROOT

2 CARROTS, PEELED AND CHOPPED

1 PARSNIP, TRIMMED AND CHOPPED

2 CUPS BROCCOLI FLORETS

2 CUPS CAULIFLOWER FLORETS

2 TABLESPOONS OLIVE OIL

DIRECTIONS

1. Place the brine in a large stockpot, add the chicken, and place it in the refrigerator overnight. If needed, weigh the chicken down so it is submerged in the brine.

2. Remove the chicken from the brine and discard the brine. Place the chicken on a wire rack resting in a baking sheet and pat as dry as possible. Let sit at room temperature for 1 hour.

3. Preheat the oven to 450°F. Place the chicken in a baking dish, season lightly with salt and pepper, and sprinkle the thyme leaves on top. Place in the oven and roast until the juices run clear and the internal temperature in the thick part of a thigh is 160°F, about 35 minutes. Remove, transfer to a wire rack, and let it rest. Leave the oven on.

4. Place the remaining ingredients in a mixing bowl, season with salt and pepper, and toss to evenly coat. Place on a parchment–lined baking sheet and roast until tender, about 25 minutes. Remove, carve the chicken, and serve alongside the roasted vegetable medley.

CHICKEN BRINE

Place ¾ cup kosher salt, 6 tablespoons sugar, 6 cups room-temperature water, 1½ teaspoons whole black peppercorns, 5 crushed garlic cloves, 3 sprigs of fresh thyme, and 1 bay leaf in a large saucepan and bring the mixture to a boil, stirring to dissolve the sugar and salt. When these are dissolved, remove the pan from heat, transfer the mixture to a stockpot, and add 12 cups ice water and 4 cups ice. Let cool to room temperature before adding the chicken.

YIELD: **6 SERVINGS**

ACTIVE TIME: **30 MINUTES**

TOTAL TIME: **1 HOUR AND 30 MINUTES**

Kofta Curry

INGREDIENTS

FOR THE DUMPLINGS

2 LBS. ZUCCHINI, TRIMMED AND GRATED

1 TABLESPOON KOSHER SALT

1 SMALL RED ONION, CHOPPED

¼ CUP RAW CASHEWS

2 GARLIC CLOVES, MINCED

1-INCH PIECE OF FRESH GINGER, PEELED AND MINCED

4 BIRD'S EYE CHILI PEPPERS, STEMMED, SEEDS AND RIBS REMOVED, AND MINCED

½ CUP CHICKPEA FLOUR

2 TABLESPOONS FINELY CHOPPED FRESH CILANTRO

VEGETABLE OIL, AS NEEDED

Continued...

DIRECTIONS

1. To begin preparations for the dumplings, place the grated zucchini in a colander, add the salt, and stir to combine. Let the zucchini sit for 20 minutes.

2. While the zucchini is sitting, begin preparations for the sauce. Place the olive oil in a saucepan and warm it over medium-high heat. When the oil starts to shimmer, add the cumin seeds, cook for about 1 minute, until they are fragrant, and then add the onion, chilies, cashews, and raisins. Sauté until the onion and cashews start to brown, about 5 minutes. Add the tomatoes and salt, cook for another 2 minutes, transfer the mixture to a food processor, and puree until smooth. Set the puree aside and resume preparations for the dumplings.

3. Place the onion, cashews, garlic, ginger, and chilies in a food processor and blitz until the mixture becomes a chunky paste.

4. Place the zucchini in a kitchen towel and wring it to remove as much liquid as possible. Place the zucchini in a mixing bowl and add the onion-and-cashew paste. Stir to combine, add the chickpea flour and cilantro, and fold to incorporate. The dough should be just slightly wet.

5. Add vegetable oil to a Dutch oven until it is about 2 inches deep and warm to 300°F. As the oil warms, form tablespoons of the dough into balls and place them on a parchment-lined baking sheet. Place the dumplings in the hot oil and fry until golden brown, about 5 minutes. Work in batches if necessary. Transfer the cooked dumplings to a paper towel–lined plate to drain and resume preparations for the sauce.

6. Return the puree to the saucepan, add the remaining ingredients, and stir to combine. Heat until warmed through, ladle into warmed bowls, and divide the dumplings between them.

FOR THE SAUCE

2 TABLESPOONS OLIVE OIL

1 TEASPOON CUMIN SEEDS

1 RED ONION, CHOPPED

4 BIRD'S EYE CHILI PEPPERS,
STEMMED, SEEDS AND RIBS
REMOVED, AND MINCED

2 TABLESPOONS RAW CASHEWS

2 TABLESPOONS GOLDEN RAISINS

1 (28 OZ.) CAN OF DICED
TOMATOES, DRAINED

1 TEASPOON KOSHER SALT

¼ CUP MILK

¼ CUP HEAVY CREAM

¼ TEASPOON TURMERIC

2 PINCHES OF BLACK PEPPER

2 PINCHES OF CINNAMON

2 PINCHES OF GROUND CLOVES

2 PINCHES OF FRESHLY GRATED
NUTMEG

2 PINCHES OF CARDAMOM

Slow-Cooker Cacciatore

INGREDIENTS

6 BONELESS, SKINLESS CHICKEN THIGHS

1 (28 OZ.) CAN OF WHOLE TOMATOES, DRAINED

1 (28 OZ.) CAN OF DICED TOMATOES, DRAINED

⅔ CUP DRY RED WINE

4 SHALLOTS, CHOPPED

3 GARLIC CLOVES, MINCED

1 GREEN BELL PEPPER, STEMMED, SEEDS AND RIBS REMOVED, AND CHOPPED

1 YELLOW BELL PEPPER, STEMMED, SEEDS AND RIBS REMOVED, AND CHOPPED

1 CUP BUTTON MUSHROOMS, CHOPPED

1½ TABLESPOONS DRIED OREGANO

1 TABLESPOON GARLIC POWDER

1 TABLESPOON SUGAR

2 TABLESPOONS KOSHER SALT, PLUS MORE TO TASTE

½ TEASPOON RED PEPPER FLAKES

BLACK PEPPER, TO TASTE

PARMESAN CHEESE, GRATED, FOR GARNISH

FRESH PARSLEY, FINELY CHOPPED, FOR GARNISH

DIRECTIONS

1. Place all of the ingredients, save the Parmesan and parsley, in a slow cooker and cook on low until the chicken is very tender, about 5½ hours. The cooking time may vary depending on your slow cooker, so be sure to check after about 4½ hours to avoid overcooking.

2. To serve, top each portion with a generous amount of Parmesan cheese and parsley.

Shakshuka with Eggs

INGREDIENTS

1 TABLESPOON OLIVE OIL

1 ONION, CHOPPED

2 GARLIC CLOVES, MINCED

½ LB. TOMATILLOS, HUSKED, RINSED, AND CHOPPED

1 (12 OZ.) PACKAGE OF FROZEN SPINACH

1 TEASPOON CORIANDER

¼ CUP WATER

SALT AND PEPPER, TO TASTE

4 EGGS

TABASCO, FOR SERVING (OPTIONAL)

DIRECTIONS

1. Place the oil in a large skillet and warm it over medium-high heat. When the oil starts to shimmer, add the onion and sauté until it starts to soften, about 5 minutes. Add the garlic and cook until fragrant, about 1 minute. Add the tomatillos and cook until they have collapsed, about 8 minutes.

2. Add the spinach, coriander, and water and cook, breaking up the spinach with a fork, until the spinach is completely defrosted and blended with the tomatillos. Season with salt and pepper.

3. Evenly spread the mixture in the pan and then make four indentations in it. Crack an egg into each indentation. Reduce the heat to medium, cover the pan, and cook until the whites of the eggs are set, 3 to 5 minutes. Serve with Tabasco, if desired.

Stuffed Tomatoes

INGREDIENTS

6 LARGE TOMATOES

SALT AND PEPPER, TO TASTE

1 TABLESPOON OLIVE OIL

1 RED ONION, CHOPPED

4 GARLIC CLOVES, MINCED

½ GREEN BELL PEPPER, STEMMED, SEEDS AND RIBS REMOVED, AND CHOPPED

½ LB. GROUND TURKEY

1 TEASPOON CUMIN

1 TEASPOON FINELY CHOPPED FRESH OREGANO

½ TEASPOON ALLSPICE

½ TEASPOON FRESHLY GRATED NUTMEG

2 TEASPOONS RED PEPPER FLAKES

½ CUP COOKED LONG-GRAIN RICE

¼ CUP FINELY CHOPPED FRESH PARSLEY

¼ CUP FINELY CHOPPED FRESH MINT

DIRECTIONS

1. Cut off the tops of the tomatoes and use a spoon to scoop out the insides. Sprinkle salt into the cavities and turn the tomatoes upside down on a paper towel–lined plate. Let them drain for 30 minutes.

2. Place the olive oil in a 12-inch cast-iron skillet and warm it over medium-high heat. When the oil starts to shimmer, add the onion, garlic, and bell pepper and sauté until the onion is translucent, about 3 minutes. Add the turkey, cumin, oregano, allspice, and nutmeg, season with salt and pepper, and cook, breaking the turkey up with a fork, until it is browned, about 8 minutes.

3. Set the oven's broiler to high. Transfer the mixture in the skillet to a mixing bowl, add the red pepper flakes, rice, parsley, and mint, and stir to combine. Fill the tomatoes' cavities with the mixture, wipe out the skillet, and arrange the tomatoes in the pan.

4. Place the stuffed tomatoes under the broiler and cook until the tops start to blister, about 5 minutes. Remove from the oven and serve immediately.

Falafel

INGREDIENTS

1½ (14 OZ.) CANS OF CHICKPEAS, DRAINED AND RINSED

1 SMALL ONION, DICED

3 GARLIC CLOVES

¼ CUP ALL-PURPOSE FLOUR

2 TABLESPOONS FINELY CHOPPED FRESH PARSLEY

1 TABLESPOON FRESH LEMON JUICE

1 TABLESPOON CORIANDER

2 TEASPOONS CUMIN

1 TEASPOON BAKING SODA

SALT AND CAYENNE PEPPER, TO TASTE

VEGETABLE OIL, AS NEEDED

PITA BREAD, FOR SERVING

HUMMUS (SEE PAGE 37), FOR SERVING

DIRECTIONS

1. Place the chickpeas in a food processor. Add the onion, garlic, flour, parsley, lemon juice, coriander, cumin, baking soda, salt, and cayenne and blitz until the mixture is a smooth paste, scraping the work bowl as necessary.

2. Form the mixture into 1-inch balls, place them on a parchment-lined baking sheet, cover tightly with plastic wrap, and refrigerate for 20 minutes.

3. Add vegetable oil to a Dutch oven until it is approximately 2 inches deep and warm to 375°F over medium-high heat. Working in batches, add the falafel and fry until browned all over, about 3 minutes. Transfer the cooked falafel to a paper towel–lined plate to drain. When all of the falafel have been cooked, serve them with pita bread and Hummus.

METRIC CONVERSIONS

U.S. Measurement	Approximate Metric Liquid Measurement	Approximate Metric Dry Measurement
1 teaspoon	5 ml	5 g
1 tablespoon or ½ ounce	15 ml	14 g
1 ounce or ⅛ cup	30 ml	29 g
¼ cup or 2 ounces	60 ml	57 g
⅓ cup	80 ml	76 g
½ cup or 4 ounces	120 ml	113 g
⅔ cup	160 ml	151 g
¾ cup or 6 ounces	180 ml	170 g
1 cup or 8 ounces or ½ pint	240 ml	227 g
1½ cups or 12 ounces	350 ml	340 g
2 cups or 1 pint or 16 ounces	475 ml	454 g
3 cups or 1½ pints	700 ml	680 g
4 cups or 2 pints or 1 quart	950 ml	908 g

INDEX

C

ABOUT CIDER MILL PRESS
BOOK PUBLISHERS

❧ ❈ ☙

Good ideas ripen with time. From seed to harvest, Cider Mill Press brings fine reading, information, and entertainment together between the covers of its creatively crafted books. Our Cider Mill bears fruit twice a year, publishing a new crop of titles each spring and fall.

"Where Good Books Are Ready for Press"

Visit us online at
cidermillpress.com
or write to us at
PO Box 454
12 Spring St.
Kennebunkport, Maine 04046